Building a Winning Team
1 Corinthians

James T. Dyet

This book has been prepared primarily for group study in connection with the Adult Teacher's Guide, available from Regular Baptist Press. A transparency packet with sixteen sheets is also available. This book may be used for individual instruction.

REGULAR BAPTIST PRESS
1300 North Meacham Road
Schaumburg, Illinois 60173-4888

In Canada: Eizenga Ministries
1564 Hillside Drive, London, Ontario N6G 4M6

About the Author

James T. Dyet is an editor and writer for Regular Baptist Press. He joined the editorial staff in early 1990. Prior to this he served for almost twenty years on the editorial staff of Accent Publications, Denver, Colorado.

Dr. Dyet completed the pastor's course at Moody Bible Institute and earned the B.A. at Houghton College. He studied at Indiana State University and holds an earned doctorate and an honorary doctorate from Baptist Christian University.

Dr. Dyet has been involved in pastoral ministry for thirty years. He has written several books as well as Sunday School curriculum. This is his second series of adult Sunday School lessons for Regular Baptist Press. His other series is titled *A Heart for Service*, based on the book of 1 Samuel.

Dr. Dyet and his wife, Gloria, reside in Streamwood, Illinois. They have three grown children.

BUILDING A WINNING TEAM
Adult Student Manual
Vol. 39, No. 3
© 1991 by Regular Baptist Press, Schaumburg, Illinois
Printed in U.S.A.
Vernon D. Miller, Executive Editor; James T. Dyet,
    Youth and Adult Editor; Annette Haskins, Assistant

Contents

Bible Book Abbreviations

The following abbreviations for Bible books are used throughout this study guide. They are listed here in alphabetical order, and, for your convenience, the full names are spelled out. We trust this will help you locate these books in your Bible as you engage in personal Bible study.

(1 Cor.)	1 Corinthians
(2 Cor.)	2 Corinthians
(Dan.)	Daniel
(Eph.)	Ephesians
(Exod.)	Exodus
(Ezek.)	Ezekiel
(Gal.)	Galatians
(Gen.)	Genesis
(Heb.)	Hebrews
(Isa.)	Isaiah
(Judg.)	Judges
(Lev.)	Leviticus
(Mal.)	Malachi
(Matt.)	Matthew
(1 Pet.)	1 Peter
(2 Pet.)	2 Peter
(Phil.)	Philippians
(Ps.)	Psalms
(Rev.)	Revelation
(Rom.)	Romans
(2 Sam.)	2 Samuel
(1 Thess.)	1 Thessalonians
(2 Thess.)	2 Thessalonians
(1 Tim.)	1 Timothy
(2 Tim.)	2 Timothy

Be a Team Player!

Occasionally, a coach explains his team's winning performance by stating, "The whole team came to play today." He means, of course, the team wanted to win and therefore played hard to achieve its goal. On the other hand, the coach of the losing team laments, "Obviously, we didn't come to play today. We need to regroup and determine to play up to our potential. We have a lot of talent on our team, but we're not using it. When we come together as a team, and everyone covers his assignment properly, we'll start winning some games."

The Corinthian church wasn't enjoying spiritual victory because its members were out of condition. They were carnal and self-centered. In 1 Corinthians Paul challenged them to become spiritually fit, unite as a team of believers, exercise their spiritual gifts, and throw themselves wholeheartedly into the work of the Lord. If they did these things, they would obtain incorruptible crowns.

In the 1990s a local church can experience victory after victory in its service for Christ, or it can founder, lose ground, and suffer defeat. The outcome depends upon the willingness of its members to become a winning team.

You can make a significant contribution to your church's success. God has given you at least one spiritual gift to use in conjunction with the spiritual gifts of your fellow believers. Employ it well. Cooperate. Be a team player.

As you study 1 Corinthians this quarter, refer often to

this study guide. Learn the assigned memory verses; read the related Scriptures; answer the questions you find in each lesson; and participate in class discussions. The more you put into your personal study of 1 Corinthians, the stronger you will grow as a Christian and the better equipped you will be to help your local church build winning team.

Problems today
 Church Division 1
 Pride, haughty spirit 2
 Lack of growth 3
   on doctrine
 Incorrect view of ministers 4
  Immorality 5
 Instability in Home 6-7
 abuse of christian liability 8
    liberty
 neglect + abuse of finances 9
 Idolatry: lack of seperation 10

acts 18 background 1-4:5
            12-17

    now AD 56 - 5 yrs later

Corinth - wicked city
600,000   Temple prostitutes
              sea port

V3 Grace from God, then peace

we lack prayer V4

Baptism not necessary for Salvation 1 Cor 1:17
V18 - Continual

1 A Plea for Unity

† 1 Corinthians 1

Believers need to be team players in their local church, grateful for their salvation and dedicated to the goal of glorifying God.

It's typical for kids to admire sports figures. A kid may hang a poster of his hero on a bedroom wall, try to get the champion's autograph, keep track of his stats, join a fan club and wear a jersey or T-shirt bearing his number and name. Even many grown-up "kids" pay similar homage to sports heroes. Probably, such admiration is harmless. It may even be helpful if the athlete is a good role model and the admiration doesn't become idolatrous.

Today, many Christians are fans of religious personalities. Each claims his radio or TV preacher or recording artist is the best. These Christians buy their heroes' books or records and tapes. They stand in long lines at autograph parties and sit mesmerized through personal appearances. Although some well-known preachers, vocalists and musicians do edify and encourage God's people, many who admire them may also idolize them and inadvertently esteem them more highly than Jesus Christ. Undoubtedly, legitimate servants of God don't welcome this attention. Such attention blurs the spiritual focus of the hero-worshipers and often weakens their loyalty to their local churches.

Corinthian Fan Clubs

Religious fan clubs are not a twentieth-century phenomenon. The apostle Paul faced a similar phenomenon in his day. Near the end of his second missionary journey, the apostle Paul wrote 1 Corinthians from Ephesus (Acts 20:31; 1 Cor. 16:5–8). He had received a report from the family of Chloe about bickering in the church (1 Cor. 1:11). Also, he had received a letter from the church, which posed a number of questions (7:1). Furthermore, a delegation from the church had paid him a visit. All these circumstances prompted Paul to write 1 Corinthians. His Spirit-inspired letter offered the church at Corinth solutions to problems, answers to questions and instructions for saintly living. It is, therefore, intensely practical for churches today, which still face many of the same issues.

Fan clubs had sprung up in the Corinthian church. This was the first problem Paul addressed. Some Christians had pledged allegiance to Paul; some to Apollos; some to Peter; and some to Christ (1 Cor. 1:12). Apparently, some must have liked Paul's emphasis on

Grow in Grace . . .

"Now I beseech you, brethren, by the name of our Lord Jesus Christ, that ye all speak the same thing, and that there be no divisions among you; but that ye be perfectly joined together in the same mind and in the same judgment" (1 Cor. 1:10).

Believers in a local church need to believe the written Word, honor the living Word, and proclaim the whole Word; and do so as a team.

... **and Knowledge**

*Read these related
Scriptures as you study*
1 Corinthians 1 *this week.*

John 1:1–12

Acts 9:1–16
Acts 17:22–32
Romans 3:23–31
Romans 5:1–8
Ephesians 1:1–12
3 John

Christian liberty; some, Apollos's eloquent preaching; and some, Peter's Jewish credentials. This cliquishness was understandably wrong, but why was it wrong to announce, "I am a follower of Christ"? In his *Letters to the Corinthians* William Barclay explains: "Their real fault was not in saying that they belonged to Christ, but in acting as if Christ belonged to them. It may well describe a little, intolerant, self-righteous group."

As long as cliques prevailed in the church, the Corinthian Christians could not serve God as a team. Intra-church competition always suffocates a spirit of cooperation and stifles spiritual growth. Unhappy is the church whose members would rather devour one another than develop one another.

Work as a Team

To help unify the Corinthian Christians, Paul directed their attention to God's grace. Paul, Apollos, Peter and all Christians were nothing apart from the grace of God. All glory belonged to the Lord. "He that glorieth, let him glory in the Lord," Paul wrote (1 Cor. 1:31). Cliques are wrong because they ascribe to human leaders glory that rightfully belongs to God. Paul reminded his readers they had been called unto the fellowship of God's Son, the Lord Jesus Christ (v. 9). "Fellowship" suggests partnership, a joint participation in a cause; in other words, a team concept. Instead of lining up behind favorite leaders, the Corinthians were advised by Paul to unite as one in the cause of Christ (v. 10).

Look What God Has Done for Us!

Paul didn't take any credit for his apostleship, and he certainly didn't want any personal glory from the "I-am-of-Paul" club at Corinth. He made it clear to the Corinthians that he was "called to be an apostle of Jesus Christ through the will of God" (v. 1a). Divine grace had turned his whole life around. Before God saved him, he was Saul the Antagonist, the disciples' enemy (Acts 9:1). After God saved him, he was Paul the Apostle, the Devil's enemy (Gal. 1:21–24)!

Still focusing on the grace of God in order to show the folly of glorifying human leaders, Paul included Sosthenes's name in the greeting (1 Cor. 1:1b). This man may have been the former synagogue leader at Corinth, who was beaten by an unruly Gentile mob (Acts 18:17). Whoever he was, Paul identified him to the Corinthian church as "our brother" (1 Cor. 1:1b). Perhaps the term "brother" would remind the Corinthian Christians that they were a family, the most closely knit team of all! Paul wanted the Corinthian church to enjoy God's grace and peace (v. 3). Grace would strengthen them, and peace would settle them.

> Q1. Read 1 Corinthians 1:1–9. *What had God done for the Corinthian Christians?*
>
> _____
>
> _____
>
> _____
>
> _____
>
> Q2. *What has God's grace accomplished in your life?*
>
> _____

_____

_____

Look to Calvary

Christians can thank God for their spiritual leaders and cooperate with them in the work of the Lord, but they must not develop a slave/master relationship with those leaders. Paul asked the Corinthians, "Is Christ divided? was Paul crucified for you? or were ye baptized in the name of Paul?" (v. 13). When a believer is baptized, he publicly professes allegiance to the One Who saved him. Christ is his Lord and Master. Apparently, in Paul's day, some Christians were showing more loyalty to their baptizers than to the Lord in Whose name they were baptized. This explains Paul's apparent downplaying of his role as a baptizer and his emphasis in his preaching of the Cross (vv. 14–17).

Q3. What causes divisions in a church?

_____

_____

Q4. What unifies a church?

_____

_____

When Paul preached about Christ's death on the cross, he spoke simply and clearly. He avoided empty rhetoric and philosophical jargon, "lest the cross of Christ should be made of none effect" (v. 17). A preacher's responsibility is to present the gospel in understandable and persuasive language. The pulpit was never intended to be a showcase where a preacher

11

displays his knowledge of unusual and almost unpronounceable words. Jesus used simple, understandable words when He preached, and His words made an impact. Mark 12:37 relates that "the common people heard him gladly." Matthew 7:28 and 29 indicate "the people were astonished at his doctrine: for he taught them as one having authority, and not as the scribes."

The Cross divides the human race into two segments. One segment consists of those who have believed on Christ, Who died on the cross for their sins. The other segment consists of those who have not believed on Christ. The world's population, then, is made up of saved sinners and unsaved sinners. A person is in one group or the other. When Jesus died at Calvary, two criminals died there too; one on His right, the other on His left. One believed on Him; the other rejected Him. There, at Calvary, was a representation of how the cross of Christ divides the whole human race.

Some unsaved sinners regard the preaching of the Cross as absolute nonsense (1 Cor. 1:18a). However, we Christians know the message of the Cross pulsates with the power of God (v. 18b). We heard the gospel, believed on Christ as Savior and passed from spiritual death unto life. We received new life—eternal life—as a gift from God through Christ, made possible by the shed blood of Christ (Rom. 3:24, 25; 5:8, 9; 6:23).

The apostle Paul knew by firsthand experience that the message of the Cross is the power of God. After years of slavish devotion to the law, he discovered salvation cannot be earned; it must be received by faith. He released his grip on all his religious credentials and by faith embraced the Cross, believing in the full sufficiency of Christ's redemptive work (Gal. 1:4; 3:11–13; Phil. 3:4–9). No wonder he exclaimed: "For I am not ashamed of the gospel of Christ: for it is the power of God unto salvation to every one that believeth; to the Jew first, and also to the Greek" (Rom. 1:16).

Big Heads and Blind Hearts

The Greeks placed a high value on philosophy and oratory. The names Socrates, Plato and Aristotle have long been associated with Greek philosophy; and the name Demosthenes with Greek oratory. However, neither the wisest secular philosophy nor the most captivating oratory can match the wisdom of God and the simple message of the Cross. Drawing from Isaiah 29:14 and 33:18, Paul informed the Corinthians that God will destroy worldly wisdom and leave worldy-wise philosophers, writers and debaters defenseless (1 Cor. 1:19, 20).

Worldly wisdom is at a loss to explain God and at a loss to find God. "The world by wisdom knew not God," Paul wrote in verse 21. The secular mind cannot philosophize its way to God. Peace with God doesn't come wrapped in a PhD diploma or attached to a debate team's 1st Prize ribbon. Even the most highly educated human beings need the simple gospel message and the Spirit's enlightenment in order to be saved by faith in Christ (v. 21). Unfortunately, the worldly-wise Gentiles had big heads—intellectual pride—and therefore rejected the gospel (v. 22).

The Jews, on the other hand, rejected the preaching of the Cross because they required a sign (v. 22). Their hearts were blind to the truth that their Messiah died on the cross as the Lamb of God. They reasoned that a crucified person was accursed of God (Deut. 21:23). A messiah, in their judgment, would be kingly and powerful. He would destroy Israel's oppressors and restore the kingdom to Israel. He would give supernatural signs to prove his messiahship.

When Jesus Christ ministered and taught in Palestine, the Jewish leaders often asked Him for signs, although His miracles should have been enough proof for them (Matt. 12:38; 16:1, 4; Mark 8:11; John 6:30).

Jesus responded that His death, burial and resurrection would serve as a sign (Matt. 12:39); but, because their hearts were blind, the Jews' rejected this sign when it occurred.

By rejecting the true Messiah, the Jews left themselves open to the claims of impostors. In A.D. 45, just a few years after Christ's death and resurrection, a false messiah by the name of Theudas persuaded thousands of Jews to leave their homes and follow him. He led them to the Jordan River and promised he would lead them across by first commanding it to divide. Of course, the river failed to oblige him. Nine years later, a self-proclaimed prophet emerged from Egypt. He led 30,000 people to the Mount of Olives. From this vantage point, they were supposed to watch him command the walls of Jerusalem to fall down. Naturally, the show fizzled!

This penchant for signs will reach full bloom in the Tribulation, when unbelieving Jews will accept the witness of the False Prophet. He will deceive them by performing wonders (Rev. 13:11–14). In their blind acceptance of the false prophet, the Jews will fulfill Jesus' prophecy: "I am come in my Father's name, and ye receive me not: if another shall come in his own name, him ye will receive" (John 5:43).

Paul did not adjust the gospel to fit either worldly-wise Gentiles or sign-seeking Jews. He preached "Christ crucified, unto the Jews a stumblingblock, and unto the Greeks foolishness" (1 Cor. 1:23). However, not all Jews stumbled over the Cross, and not all Gentiles thought the message of the Cross was foolish; Paul declared: "But unto them which are called, both Jews and Greeks, Christ the power of God, and the wisdom of God" (v. 24).

Christ's death on the cross seemed foolish to the worldly-wise, and to the Jews it was a stumbling block, but in that death God demonstrated infinite power and wisdom. His "foolishness" was wiser than human wisdom, and His "weakness" was stronger than human strength (vv. 24, 25). The crucifixion proved God's power to save sinners and His wisdom in providing for sinners the only suitable representative of both God and man. As the "one mediator between God and men" (1 Tim. 2:5), Christ Jesus, the God-Man, reconciled God and sinners. As a result, all who believe on Him as Savior receive forgiveness and peace with God.

> Q5. How does it encourage you to know that "the foolishness of God is wiser than men; and the weakness of God is stronger than men" (1 Cor. 1:25)?

_____

_____

_____

God's Amazing Minority

Abraham Lincoln commented that the Lord must love common people because He made so many of them. We can push his comment further by observing that God must love common people because He made so many of them Christians. It certainly seems characteristic of God in all periods of church history to have saved mainly common people. Around A.D. 178 Celcus, a bitter critic of Christianity, wrote about Christians: "We see them in their own houses, wool dressers, cobblers and fullers, the most uneducated and vulgar persons." He compared Christians to "a swarm of bats—or ants creeping out of their nests—or frogs holding a symposium round a swamp—or worms in conventicle in a corner of mud."

A few affluent, powerful, brilliant Christians may have been in the church at Corinth, but most were ordinary people saved by extraordinary grace. God called

15

into the fellowship of His Son mainly common people so they couldn't boast about their wisdom, authority, talents or money. Their boasting had to be about what the Lord had done for them, in spite of their humble status (vv. 27–29). In lifting their favorite leaders onto pedestals, the Corinthian Christians were ignoring the fact that men were nothing apart from the grace of God! Only God deserved the glory the Corinthians were ascribing to their leaders.

All Things in Jesus

Martin Luther exclaimed, "Man only needs Jesus Christ!" He was right. In Christ, believers find "wisdom, and righteousness, and sanctification, and redemption" (v. 30). Although a little girl misquoted Psalm 23:1 in Sunday Bible School, her words make sense. "The Lord is my shepherd," she said, "I've got all I want." Having all things in Jesus, shouldn't we glory in the Lord (1 Cor. 1:31) and team up with fellow believers to serve Him?

Time for Action

• You've been called into "the fellowship of his Son Jesus Christ our Lord" (1 Cor. 1:9). What will you do today to enhance your personal fellowship with Christ?

• How can you help develop the team concept in your church?

• In simple, clear language tell someone this week how to be saved.

• If you are part of a clique, why not take a positive step toward broader fellowship in your church?

• Praise the Lord for each of the following: wisdom, righteousness, sanctification and redemption (1 Cor. 1:30).

2 God's Reliable Word

† 1 Corinthians 2

The Bible is God's inspired and fully reliable Word.

What does a church want most in a pastor—good looks? loads of charm? a sparkling personality? middle thirties with thirty years pastoral experience? a humble wife with outstanding musical ability? kids that are smart but not too smart? loyalty to God's Word and the ability to teach and preach it forcefully and clearly? Perhaps none of the above or all of the above fit some churches' demands.

The apostle Paul wouldn't be well received by churches today that judge a man's worth by the way he combs his hair or charms a crowd. Apparently, Paul's appearance was less than a knockout, and his approach to problems was sometimes more direct than diplomatic. But Paul loved God and His people. He also loved the Word of God, and he declared it humbly, forcefully and clearly.

A Slow Start

When Paul stepped inside Corinth's city limits, he felt uneasy. Reflecting on the experience, he told the Corinthian believers: "I was with you in weakness, and in fear, and in much trembling" (1 Cor. 2:3). Corinth wasn't the kind of city that would roll out a red carpet for a preacher. It was a vile, crime-ridden big city. Thievery, drunkenness and prostitution flourished, and so did pagan practices. The temple of Aphrodite (the goddess of love) stood on a high hill, beckoning Corinthians to its halls. Corinth had such a vile reputation that, if a Corinthian was depicted in a Greek play, he was shown drunk.

Paul was tired and discouraged when he came to Corinth. He had recently encountered more than enough opposition to tempt anyone to throw in the towel and return home. Certain men had stirred up trouble for him at Philippi (Acts 16:19–24). At Thessalonica Jews sparked a riot against him (Acts 17:5–8). At Berea Paul had endured similar trouble, when the angry Jews from Thessalonica arrived and incited the city against him (v. 13). Things hadn't gone well at Athens either. Only a few in that proud, intellectual city believed (vv. 32–34). Other circumstances also threatened to discourage Paul. He was probably alone when he reached Corinth. His coworkers, Silas and Timothy, were in Macedonia. Also, the Corinthians had a low opinion of his appearance and speech (2 Cor. 10:10). So we can understand why Paul was somewhat

Grow in Grace . . .

"For the prophecy came not in old time by the will of man: but holy men of God spake as they were moved by the Holy Ghost" (2 Pet. 1:21).

The Bible is not simply a carefully written human document. It is the product of divine inspiration. It is the Word of God.

. . . and Knowledge

*Read these related
Scriptures as you study
1 Corinthians 2 this week.*

Psalm 1
Psalm 19
Ezekiel 2:1–7
2 Timothy 3:14–17
2 Peter 1:15–21

discouraged when he entered Corinth. However, when Silas and Timothy rejoined him there, he took heart and preached, first to the Jews, then to the Gentiles (Acts 18:5).

Q1. What discourages you in your work for the Lord?

_____

_____

_____

Q2. What encourages you in your work for the Lord?

_____

_____

_____

Single-minded Preaching

Paul's preaching was precise. He had made up his mind to stick to the subject of "Jesus Christ, and him crucified" (1 Cor. 2:2). He could have crusaded against any number of social ills, because there were so many in Corinth, but he chose to limit his preaching to the redemptive work of Christ at Calvary. This was a wise decision. Social reform without personal regeneration is a poor substitute for what God wants to accomplish. He wants to change sinners by saving them and giving them brand-new lives. If enough residents of a community become Christians, the community will begin to change, resulting in less crime, fewer injustices, less fear, fewer broken homes and less hatred. Someone observed:

> Since Jesus came into the town,
>   the Devil's been wearing a frown.
> Many lives have been changed,
>   many homes rearranged,
> Since Jesus came into the town.

In preaching to the Corinthians, Paul didn't use superior language or philosophical wisdom. He simply declared "the testimony of God"—the gospel (1 Cor. 2:1). He didn't want to showcase himself but rather the gospel. Abstract terms and unfamiliar words would obstruct the message of the Cross and confuse the listeners. So he rejected both and proclaimed Christ in simple, forthright language (vv. 1, 4a). He knew the Spirit of God would honor humble preaching that focused on Christ. Indeed, the Holy Spirit did honor Paul's preaching. The Spirit's power accompanied Paul's message, and people believed on Christ. Their faith was anchored in "Thus saith the Lord" and not in persuasive speech and human wisdom (v. 5).

Q3. What persuaded you to become a Christian?

_____

_____

Real Wisdom

When Satan tempted Eve in the garden in Eden, he appealed to her interest in being as wise as God. He urged her to eat of the tree of knowledge of good and evil by telling her, "God doth know that in the day ye eat thereof, then your eyes shall be opened, and ye shall be as gods, knowing good and evil" (Gen. 3:5).

Eve bit into this bait. Genesis 3:6 reports: "And when the woman [Eve] saw that the tree was good for food, and that it was pleasant to the eyes, and a tree to be desired to make one wise, she took of the fruit thereof, and did eat, and gave also unto her husband with her; and he did eat."

Since that day in Eden, the human race has had a love affair with worldly wisdom. Unregenerate society considers itself too wise and sophisticated to believe the Bible. Human wisdom rejects the Genesis account of creation in favor of evolution, denies the supernatural in favor of higher criticism, and rejects the Cross in favor of a humanistic sense of self-importance. Unregenerate members of society neither have room for Jonah in the belly of a great fish nor for Jesus in their hearts. They feel they are too intelligent to believe such an old book as the Bible.

Q4. Do you think it's possible to sweep away all objections to the Bible by debating intelligently in the Bible's defense? Why or why not?

_____

_____

_____

Paul knew all about the world's love affair with its own kind of wisdom. He also knew God's wisdom is true and the world's is false. Only born-again persons—"them that are perfect" (1 Cor. 2:6)—understand the wisdom God employed in planning our redemption in Christ before the world began (v. 7). If the rulers of this age had accepted God's wisdom, they would not have crucified the Lord of glory (v. 8).

God's Wisdom Revealed by the Spirit

Left to his own devices, a human being would never

perceive spiritual truth. This is what Paul told the Corinthian church in 1 Corinthians 2:9, as he quoted rather freely from Isaiah 64:4. Neither the scientific method nor superior human insight can uncover what God has prepared in Christ for believers. However, the Holy Spirit has made these blessings known to believers (1 Cor. 2:10). He has disclosed to us such truths as redemption, justification and sanctification, all of which are ours in Christ. Obviously, the Holy Spirit is the perfect Agent to disclose the things of God to us, because, as Deity, He has perfect knowledge of the mind of God (v. 11).

God's Word Communicated

Before leaving the Upper Room to keep His rendezvous with death, Jesus told His disciples: "But the Comforter, which is the Holy Ghost, whom the Father will send in my name, he shall teach you all things, and bring all things to your remembrance, whatsoever I have said unto you" (John 14:26). The Holy Spirit fulfilled this promise by superintending the apostles in the writing of the New Testament.

Referring to this ministry of the Spirit, Peter wrote in 2 Peter 1:21 that "holy men of God spake as they were moved by the Holy Spirit." Paul claimed this important ministry of the Holy Spirit for himself and the other apostles. He informed the Corinthians: "Now we have received, not the spirit of the world, but the spirit which is of God; that we might know the things that are freely given to us of God. Which things also we speak, not in the words which man's wisdom teacheth, but which the Holy Ghost teacheth; comparing spiritual things with spiritual" (1 Cor. 2:12, 13).

The Holy Spirit guided the writers of Scripture in their selection of the very words God wanted in the Bible. They were His words, breathed out by Him. Second Timothy 3:16 indicates, "All scripture is given by inspiration of God [God-breathed], and is profitable for doctrine, for reproof, for correction, for instruction in righteousness."

Since "all" Scripture is God-breathed, we may conclude that even the words of Scripture are God's words. Paul alluded to this in his insistence that his words were "words . . . which the Holy Ghost teacheth" (1 Cor. 2:13). The doctrine of verbal inspiration subscribes to this important belief that divine inspiration extends even to the words of Scripture.

Plenary inspiration is a doctrinal term that identifies all the parts of Scripture as God-breathed. It views every part of Scripture as inspired as the rest of Scripture. First Chronicles may not be read as widely and enjoyably as the Gospel of John, but it is just as inspired as the Gospel of John!

> Q5. How can a Christian be strengthened spiritually by reading Old Testament books such as 1 and 2 Chronicles?
>
> _____
>
> _____
>
> _____

Because the Bible is fully inspired, it is authoritative for our beliefs and behavior. It is also reliable, infallible and inerrant. Although liberal theologians deny that the Bible is the Word of God, and neoorthodox theologians claim it is merely a human product that can become the Word of God as it speaks to a reader, we can depend upon it as the written Word of God. The Bible stands entirely and eternally as God's written Word!

God's Word Comprehended

We should not expect unsaved persons to understand Biblical truths. Paul told the Corinthians, "But the natural man receiveth not the things of the Spirit of God: for they are foolishness unto him: neither can he know them, because they are spiritually discerned" (1 Cor. 2:14).

Commenting on the condition of the natural man, H. A. Ironside wrote:

When God created man, somebody has well said, he was like a three-story house; the lower story, the body; the second-story, the soul, the seat of his natural instincts and emotions; and the third-story, the spirit, the highest part of man by which he could look up to God. But when man sinned, there was a moral earthquake, and the top-story fell down into the basement, and that leaves him a physical man, it leaves the soul in the preeminent place instead of the spirit. When you remember that the soul is the seat of man's emotional nature, you will realize that the natural man is a creature led not by conscience, not by an enlightened spirit, but following the desires of his own heart as a soulish man because he follows his own affections and desires. . . . The natural man, therefore, is the man who lives the self-life, the man whose spirit has never been quickened into newness of life; it is still down there a captive in the basement, if you will" (*Addresses on the First Epistle to the Corinthians*).

In one of the Epcot exhibits in Orlando, Florida, visitors may view a nature film. But they need 3-D glasses to see what is projected onto the screen. The glasses make the images on the screen stand out in lifelike appearance. Until a person becomes a Christian, he is like an Epcot visitor without 3-D glasses; he cannot see what God has projected in the Bible. However, when he becomes a Christian, the Holy Spirit gives him spiritual vision, and he begins to see the spiritual truths God's Word teaches (v. 15). Is it any wonder the psalmist exclaimed: "Open thou mine eyes, that I may behold wondrous things out of thy law" (Ps. 119:18)?

You're a Puzzle to Many

Although a Christian can discern spiritual truth, he is a riddle to the unsaved (1 Cor 2:15). They cannot explain what has happened to the Christian to make him think and act as he does. The unsaved may try to persuade Christians to abandon their beliefs, but they are arguing with the wrong source. God is the source of our beliefs. We accept what He has communicated to us in the Bible. As Christians, we believe what God has said in the Bible. In that sense, "we have the mind of Christ" (v. 16).

The Bible is God's reliable Word. The Holy Spirit uses it to teach sinners how to be saved and Christians how to do the will of God. Second Timothy 3:15 claims the Scriptures impart wisdom unto salvation, and 3:17 claims the Scriptures provide all we need to be spiritually mature and effectively equipped for serving God. We cannot fail if we cherish and obey this inspired, life-changing Book!

Time for Action

• Read God's Word daily. As you do so, write in a notebook what you learn about your relationship to God, to your fellow Christians and to non-Christians.

• How clearly can you explain God's plan of salvation? Using no more than fifty words, write the plan of salvation. Share your brief essay with another Christian. Revise, if necessary, then use what you wrote in a witnessing experience.

3 The Church's One Foundation

† 1 Corinthians 3

Believers are fellow ministers in the Lord's work.

It must get lonely in a baseball outfield. Infielders play close enough to one another to talk it up—to encourage one another. But who encourages an outfielder? He's way back there, all by himself, separated from the infield and the rest of the outfield. Yet an outfielder is an essential member of the team. Without his position, the team would be in serious trouble.

If you work in the church's nursery, counsel at camp, prepare the Sunday bulletin, clean the church or work in children's church, at times you may feel as lonely as an outfielder. Nevertheless, you are an important member of the total church team. Without your efforts, the church's ministry would suffer.

Your Personal Best

For the good of the team, a player strives to be at his best. He trains hard, practices hard and plays hard. He sets goals and tries to extend himself to reach what he calls "his personal best," his peak performance. In writing to the church at Corinth, Paul rebuked the believers for falling far below their personal best. Instead of striving for spiritual excellence, they were grossly

27

out of shape. They were still carrying a lot of baby fat in their spiritual lives, when they should have been strong and trim (1 Cor. 3:1). Paul told them he had to milk-feed them because they couldn't digest the meat of the Word (v. 2). Furthermore, they were acting like spoiled babies. Each had to have his own way. They fought and fussed over personalities (v. 3). They stayed in their own little groups instead of uniting as one to score spiritual victories. There was the Paul group, and there was the Apollos group, for example (v. 4). A strong challenge from Coach Paul was in order!

Q1. Name some indicators of spiritual strength.

_____

_____

_____

To God Be the Glory

Although Paul was an apostle, his hat size stayed the same because his heart was humble. He considered himself a servant of Jesus Christ. He put this into perspective for the Corinthians. "Who then is Paul, and who is Apollos," he asked (v. 5a), "but ministers by whom ye believed, even as the Lord gave to every man" (v. 5b).

Grow in Grace . . .

"For we are labourers together with God: ye are God's husbandry, ye are God's building" (1 Cor. 3:9).

What are you doing for God with His help? Meditate upon 1 Corinthians 3:9 this week.

. . . and Knowledge

Read these related Scriptures as you study **1 Corinthians 3** *this week.*

Nehemiah 4
Psalm 133
2 Corinthians 5:9–15
Galatians 5:14–26
Galatians 6:1–10
Revelation 3:7–13

Paul held a team concept of Christian service. He, Apollos, Peter and other leaders were simply God's servants, each doing what God had assigned to him. As far as Paul was concerned, God's work required a variety of ministries, but ultimately God alone produced the spiritual results (vv. 6, 7).

Paul compared his ministry and Apollos's to the labor of two workers in a garden. Paul had planted the seed of God's Word at Corinth; Apollos had watered the seed. In garden work, planting and watering aren't competitive endeavors; they are cooperative endeavors—one complements the other. Seed needs water, but it's pointless to water where seed hasn't been planted. Of course, without God's providential blessing, even properly watered seed can't germinate, grow and produce. Similarly, nothing could be accomplished for God without His guidance and enabling. The glory, therefore, is not the workers' but God's (v. 7). Clearly, the Corinthian Christians needed to develop Paul's team concept for their ministry. "We are labourers together with God," Paul wrote (v. 9a).

> Q2. *Recognizing we can only serve God with strength He gives (Phil. 4:13), what is our responsibility in working together with God?*

_____

_____

_____

29

The Right Foundation

When our daughter Heather and her husband, Brad, were building their house southwest of Denver, Colorado, they sent a tiny piece of concrete to my wife and me in Illinois. They had taken it from the foundation so we would have a souvenir of their house. Obviously, they considered the foundation a significant part of the structure. And rightly so! A house needs a strong foundation; otherwise the whole structure stands in jeopardy.

Paul called the Corinthian Christians "God's building" (v. 9b). Knowing the importance of a strong foundation, Paul had laid the right foundation in Corinth when he had preached there several years earlier. He identified the foundation as Jesus Christ (v. 11).

Years ago, an expensive new house in northern Virginia split wide open from the bottom to the top. It hadn't been struck by lightning. It fell victim to the ground it rested on, ground that was sandy and spring-fed. The ground shifted, and so did the house. Instantly the single family dwelling became a duplex without a dividing wall!

A church must stand on the Rock of Ages. All other ground is spiritual quicksand.

The Right Building Materials

In addition to resting on the foundation of Christ Jesus, a church must also grow strong on that foundation. As builders, Christian workers must select their building materials wisely. "Let every man take heed how he buildeth thereupon," Paul cautioned (v. 10b). The choice is between materials that last and materials that don't last. "Gold, silver, precious stones" (v. 12) are valuable and durable. "Wood, hay, stubble" (v. 12) are consumable and practically worthless.

Paul's challenge to the Corinthians is appropriate

for us too. Each of us has a responsibility to build up fellow believers. Ephesians 4:16 states: "From whom [Christ] the whole body fitly joined together and compacted by that which every joint supplieth, according to the effectual working in the measure of every part, maketh increase of the body unto the edifying of itself in love." We build with the right materials if we use our spiritual gifts faithfully, in love, in dependence upon the Holy Spirit and for God's glory (Rom. 12:6–9; 1 Cor. 4:2; 10:31; 1 Pet. 4:10; Gal. 5:16, 22, 23).

Q3. Is it possible to perform Christian service in a sinful way? Explain.

_____

_____

_____

Motives are crucial in Christian service. A person may work hard and long to build a big Sunday Bible School class or a big church, but if his motive is to glorify himself, he is building with wood, hay and stubble. On the other hand, if he works faithfully and diligently out of love for Christ and to glorify God, he is building with gold, silver and precious stones.

Building Inspection

Anyone who has built a house knows about building codes and building inspectors. Often, a builder can't begin a new phase of construction until a building inspector approves the electrical work or the plumbing. Someday, every Christian's works will be inspected. This will occur at the Judgment Seat of Christ. Jesus Christ, Who is all-seeing and all-knowing, will conduct the inspection. Second Corinthians 5:10 promises "we must all appear before the judgment seat of Christ; that every one may receive the things done in his body, according to that he hath done, whether it be good or bad." First Corinthians 3:13 puts it this way: "Every man's work shall be made manifest: for the day shall declare it, because it shall be revealed by fire; and the fire shall try every man's work of what sort it is."

You may be serving the Lord in a behind-the-scenes ministry in your church. You may be wondering if anyone is aware of your contribution. You may wonder if the ministry is worth the time and effort you put into it. Look ahead to the Judgment Seat. Paul encourages: "If any man's work abide which he hath built thereupon, he shall receive a reward" (1 Cor. 3:14). The Lord rewards faithful workers, even those who work behind the scenes!

Those who refuse to work and those who perform labor with impure motives will suffer loss at the Judgment Seat of Christ. Nevertheless, they will not lose their salvation, because their sins were judged at Calvary. Paul wrote: "If any man's work shall be burned, he shall suffer loss: but he himself shall be saved; yet so as by fire" (v. 15).

A Magnificent Temple

Paul told the Corinthian believers they were the temple of God, and God's Spirit dwelled in them (v. 16). In spite of the Corinthians' carnality, they were God's people. He dwelled in them, and in doing so gave them a holy character (v. 17). Anyone who destroyed this magnificent temple would fall under God's judgment (v. 17). This was a clear warning to those who were causing dissension in the church at Corinth. It is also a clear warning today!

Q4. In your opinion, what are the leading causes of dissension in a church?

Wise Up!

Quoting Job 5:13 and Psalm 94:11, Paul attacked the worldly wisdom used by divisive ringleaders in the Corinthian church (vv. 18–20). They thought they were wise in establishing their own criteria for evaluating and ranking leaders. But God invited them to put aside worldly wisdom and become fools by comparison. This would prepare them for lessons from God about true wisdom (v. 18).

In seeking a pastoral candidate, a church must be sensitive to the Lord's will in the matter. Church members may be divided about the kind of pastor the church needs. Some may try to restrict the choice to a pastor under the age of 50. Some may insist that he be an outstanding communicator. Others may clamor for a pastor with a ThD. Still others may campaign for a sophisticated man. While it isn't wrong to want a pastor whose strengths meet the church's perceived needs, church's members must bow to the sovereignty of God. He knows best. His choice of a pastor may be different from what some want, but it is the wise choice. For example, a pastor whose age is above or below the pulpit committee's established age range may be God's choice for a church. Spiritual wisdom will persuade a humble and prayerful congregation to call him.

Q5. What qualities are essential in a pastor? See 1 Timothy 3:1–7 and Titus 1:5–9.

_____

_____

_____

_____

_____

_____

Look Up!

Paul wanted the Corinthian church to look beyond human leaders and see that only God deserves glory, honor and loyalty. "Therefore let no man glory in men," he wrote (1 Cor. 3:21a). Spiritual leaders are simply gifts from God, just as other spiritual blessings are His gifts (vv. 21b, 22). A church can appreciate its leaders, but it must not adulate them. It must worship the Giver instead of the gifts. In the final analysis every believer belongs to Christ, and Christ belongs to God (v. 23).

Q6. What's the difference between respecting a pastor and reverencing him?

_____

_____

_____

Time for Action

• Improve your spiritual progress by investing more time in Bible study and life application.

• Pray for fellow workers in your church, thanking God for them.

• Send thank-you notes to some behind-the-scenes workers in your church.

• Evaluate your Christian service. Are your motives pure? Are you a team player?

4 Just Be Faithful!

† 1 Corinthians 4

The believer is to be a faithful servant of God.

The first recorded words of Jesus are "I must be about my Father's business" (Luke 2:49). At the end of His earthly ministry, He exclaimed on the cross, "It is finished" (John 19:30). Jesus' committed His whole life to doing the will of God, and He performed God's will fully and flawlessly. Paul, too, committed his life to the task of doing what God wanted him to do. On the road to Damascus, where he first met Christ, Paul prayed, "Lord, what wilt thou have me to do?" (Acts 9:6). At the end of his life he testified, "I have fought a good fight, I have finished my course, I have kept the faith" (2 Tim. 4:7). Our Lord and Paul set examples for us to follow. Each of us has only one life to live, and we can invest it wisely by faithfully doing God's will.

Rowers and Business Managers

Although Paul was an apostle, he never let that high office go to his head. He regarded himself as a humble servant of Christ. In 1 Corinthians 4:1 he appealed to his readers to consider him and the other apostles as "the ministers of Christ" and "stewards of the mysteries of God."

35

Q1. What did Paul mean by "ministers" and "stewards"?

_____

_____

_____

The word Paul used for "ministers" means "under-rowers" and describes ship slaves who manned the ship's bottom row of oars. They pulled the oars with all their might as their master barked out the cadence. Paul's choice of this word emphasized his humility and also his submissiveness to Jesus Christ as Lord.

To understand the meaning of the word "stewards," we need to know something about the ancient world's business practices. Usually a steward served as a household's business manager. Having received a carte blanche from his master, he functioned as personnel manager, paymaster, purchasing agent and treasurer.

Paul compared his role and that of the other apostles to a steward's role. He wrote, "Let a man so account of us, as . . . stewards of the mysteries of God" (v. 1). He believed God had disclosed to them previously veiled truths about the gospel and the Church. Furthermore,

---

Grow in Grace . . .

"Moreover it is required in stewards, that a man be found faithful" (1 Cor. 4:2).

stewards: household business managers

God has committed the gospel and spiritual gifts to every Christian, and He requires each of us to be faithful in the care and use of all that He has entrusted to us.

. . . and Knowledge

Read these related Scripturtes as you study 1 Corinthians 4 this week.

Genesis 41:37–49
Luke 12:41–48
2 Corinthians 4:1–11
Philippians 2:19–30
Revelation 2:1–11

just as a steward's biggest responsibility was to be "faithful" (v. 2)—reliable, trustworthy—so Paul was fully committed to the tasks of safeguarding and dispensing the truths God had given him.

Q2. What specific doctrines has the Lord entrusted to our church?

_____

_____

_____

_____

_____

Few Christians can afford to hire a household employee to perform the kinds of duties a steward performed. Yet we can appreciate the importance of faithfulness in a house sitter. For example, if you hired someone to house-sit while you went on vacation, you would expect to find everything in good shape when you returned. However, an unreliable house sitter might break dishes, trash your house or let the bathtub overflow. To say the least, you would be annoyed with the house sitter, and perhaps you would be unwilling to pay him. You certainly wouldn't give him a bonus! Similarly, the Lord has entrusted every Christian with the gospel, with Biblical truth and with the responsibility to edify fellow believers. When He returns, will He declare us reliable and reward us?

The Perfect Judge

The Corinthian Christians failed to see that God gives His servants different abilities for a team ministry. Each person had a distinct contribution to make to the success of the church in Corinth. It was wrong, then, to place a high value on one leader to the discrediting of another. Knowing the Corinthians' perspective was out of focus, Paul wasn't flustered by their opinion of him. He knew their opinion—and even his own self-evaluation—mattered little. What truly mattered was God's opinion (vv. 3, 4). Instead of price-tagging God's servants, it was best to trust the Lord to judge their worth. He will do this when He comes for the Church. His evaluation will examine even the motives behind the deeds. Paul wrote: "Therefore judge nothing before the time, until the Lord come, who both will bring to light the hidden things of darkness, and will make manifest the counsels of the hearts" (v. 5a).

Why does a person teach a Sunday Bible School class or serve as a deacon or sing in the choir or perform some other service in church? If he does it out of love for the Lord, with a faithful servant's heart, in dependence upon the Holy Spirit and to glorify the Lord, he will receive "praise of God" (v. 5b). However, he will not receive the Lord's approval if he serves with a selfish motive. Unfortunately, a person may accept a teaching position because he wants to enhance his image in the church. Another may become a deacon in order to gain authority over others. And another may sing in the choir to be noticed and applauded. Often such sinful motives go undetected in this life, but the Lord will uncover them at His judgment seat.

Those who serve the Lord with pure motives can become discouraged. Unkind criticism, lack of visible results and the required time and effort can give any dedicated Christian second thoughts about continuing at his post, but the Lord's approval will make it all worthwhile.

Kings and Peasants

Paul had used himself and Apollos as examples of ministers and stewards who should not have been subjected to the Corinthians' faulty judgment (v. 6). But what he wrote about himself and Apollos also applied to the whole church. The Corinthian Christians needed to stop scrutinizing and rejecting some leaders while idolizing others. This conduct catered to pride and caused divisions in the church (v. 6b).

Christians must not boast about their Christian service abilities. God equips His people as He deems best for the good of His work. We owe all that we have to Him. He gave each of us distinct spiritual gifts to use alongside fellow Christians in the work of the ministry. Just as a team can't thrive if its members compete among themselves for personal glory, so a church can't succeed if its members compete for personal glory. Paul cautioned the Corinthians: "For who maketh thee to differ from another? and what hast thou that thou didst not receive? now if thou didst receive it, why dost thou glory, as if thou hadst not received it?" (v. 7).

The Corinthians' pride and worldly approach had blinded their minds to the fact that all of life is a stewardship. They indulged their fleshly appetites and pursued a materialistic lifestyle. They were living like kings (v. 8a). Paul wanted them to live like *spiritual* kings, enjoying God's blessings and honoring Him with their time, abilities and finances (v. 8b).

The apostles lived like peasants in contrast to the Corinthians' luxurious lifestyle. Like the final group thrown to hungry lions in an outdoor theater, the apostles were marching into the jaws of death as Heaven and earth watched (v. 9). They were considered "fools for Christ's sake," weak and despised; but the Corinthian Christians viewed themselves as wise, strong and highly esteemed (v. 10). The apostles experienced hunger, thirst, nakedness, beatings and homelessness (v. 11). At times they eked out a living by performing manual labor (v. 12a). When reviled, they blessed their adversaries, and they endured persecution without throwing in the towel (v. 12b). They answered insults with kind words, and they were often treated like garbage (v. 13).

Fatherly Love

Why did Paul paint such a stark contrast between his situation and that of the Corinthian Christians? Did he want to launch them on a guilt trip? No. He simply wanted to warn them about their unhealthy attitudes and divisive conduct, just as any loving father warns his children about the error of their ways (v. 14). He felt a special closeness to the believers in Corinth. He was their spiritual father because the Lord had used him to lead them to Christ. Even ten thousand caregivers in Christ couldn't take Paul's place as the Corinthians' spiritual father (v. 15).

If you have led someone to Christ, you understand Paul's loving concern for the Corinthians. You know how you long to see your spiritual offspring grow in Christ. If he strays from a Scriptural course of behavior, you grieve and counsel him to get back on course.

In many respects, discipling a new Christian is like parenting. When a child gets ill or hurt, the parent suffers too. Often a parent's love for a hurting child will make him wish he could suffer the hurt for the child. The parent can't wait to see his child well and active again. Paul longed to see the Corinthian believers leading healthy spiritual lives.

Follow the Leader

Since Paul's life was beyond reproach, he could urge

his readers to imitate him (v. 16). Paul could implore his readers to follow him because he followed Jesus Christ. Later in 1 Corinthians he wrote: "Be ye followers of me, even as I also am of Christ" (11:1). Paul would not lead his readers astray; he was walking in the steps of the Master.

In order to help the Corinthians imitate him, Paul had sent Timothy to them. He trusted Timothy implicitly. Timothy was Paul's "beloved son," and he was "faithful in the Lord" (v. 17a). Paul had led this young man to Christ and had discipled him. Timothy had emerged from this discipleship training as a devoted and trustworthy servant of Christ. As such, he would disciple the Corinthians in the Christian life and doctrine in the tradition he had learned from Paul (v. 17b).This would get them moving in the right direction—away from worldly wisdom and divisiveness and toward humility, cooperation and victory. They would find they could accomplish more for God as a unified team than as feuding cliques.

> Q3. Read 1 Timothy 4:12. *In what areas of life did Paul tell Timothy to be an example? How can you be an example in these same areas?*

_____

_____

_____

_____

_____

Can you picture what might happen in a busy city if pranksters changed the directional signs on major streets? For example, motorists accustomed to traveling a one-way street in a certain direction might experience a dramatic encounter with traffic flowing toward them. In a sense, Christians are supposed to function as directional signs, pointing the way to Christ and a holy life. If Christians in a community act in a carnal manner, bickering with one another and behaving in an unholy fashion, how will the unsaved find their way to Christ? We can readily understand the need for clear, Christlike leadership in first-century Corinth and in our communities today.

Paddle or Peace?

Depending upon their personal biases, people read situations differently. Those who respected and loved Paul must have accepted Timothy's visit as proof of Paul's concern for them. Those who opposed Paul interpreted Timothy's visit as a sign of weakness on Paul's part. They smugly concluded they could live as they pleased without Paul's intervention. Paul wrote: "Now some [of you] are puffed up, as though I would not come to you" (1 Cor. 4:18).

Paul set the record straight. Before long, if the Lord willed, he would arrive in Corinth. He would find out firsthand whether his smug critics were all talk and no walk (v. 19). He assured the Corinthians that "the kingdom of God is not in word, but in power" (v. 20). Obviously, God isn't impressed with human boasting; He looks for spiritual fruit in the lives of all who profess to know Him. The boasters at Corinth must have bragged about their loose living, but they would find out God chastens His erring children (Prov. 3:12; Heb. 12:6; Rev. 3:19).

Like every wise and faithful father, Paul loved his spiritual children enough to discipline them. He gave them a clear choice. If they continued in their sin, he would get out the "paddle" and discipline them. If they repented, he would withhold apostolic discipline. Instead of "paddling" them, he would relate to them in a loving, gentle manner (v. 21).

Paul was a faithful steward and minister of Christ.

He safeguarded what the Lord had committed to him, and he faithfully challenged the Corinthian Christians to follow Christ faithfully. If we neglect the responsibilities we have received from the Lord, we'll forfeit joy now and rewards at the Judgment Seat of Christ. How can we avoid such tragic losses? Just be faithful!

Time for Action

• Consider what the Lord has entrusted to you, and thank Him for the privilege of being a "steward."

• What Christian service opportunities do you have? List these on a sheet of paper. At the end of this week place a checkmark beside each one you fulfilled faithfully.

• Examine the driving motives in your life. What motivates you to serve Christ? What motivates you to do things that displease the Lord? In dependence upon the Holy Spirit, deal with any wrong motives you find.

• Paul suffered for the cause of Christ. Are you willing to forego personal comfort, if necessary, in order to advance the gospel?

• Do you know of someone you should disciple? Take at least the first step in this spiritual venture. Contact this person and arrange a convenient time and place to begin the process.

• Is your Heavenly Father disciplining you? If so, why not confess and forsake the sin that required this disciplinary action? God wants to put away the "paddle" even more than you do.

5 It's a Tough Job, but . . .

† 1 Corinthians 5

The local church should be pure.

If he's a member of your church, you couldn't pay me to attend your services." Such a statement may be unfounded and simply a lame excuse for not going to church. But it may also reveal the kind of damage a sinning church member inflicts on the cause of Christ. No one except God can know how many people have rejected Christ because of the sinful conduct of professing Christians in the church. Not only is the church to reach out with the gospel of Christ, it is to reveal the graces of Christ. The fruit of the Spirit ought to be evident in our lives so the unsaved can see the reality of Christ in our hearts.

Below the Rating Scale

If someone outside the Corinthian church had been asked to evaluate the effectiveness of the Corinthian church's testimony on a scale of 0 to 10, probably the score would have registered a minus 2. You see, all over town people were talking about a scandal in the church. As a matter of fact, the unsaved Corinthians seemed to be appalled by the sin, whereas the Christians were apathetic about it. The Christians were too focused on their assets—knowledge, eloquence, spiritual gifts—to be concerned about such a liability as sin in their church. Paul wrote in 1 Corinthians 5:1 and 2: "It is reported commonly that there is fornication among you, and such fornication as is not so much as named among the Gentiles, that one should have his father's wife. And ye are puffed up, and have not rather mourned, that he that hath done this deed might be taken away from among you."

Don't Ignore Sin

It isn't easy to deal with sin in the church. Often, the guilty member has relatives and friends in the church, and someone advises, "Discipline him, and you'll touch off a mass exodus from the church." The strongest argument in favor of exercising church discipline is simply this: God's Word demands it.

How did Paul find out about the unchecked sin in the church at Corinth? Perhaps the house of Chloe reported it to him just as they had informed him of the factions (1 Cor. 1:11). Possibly, the gossip had leaped

Grow in Grace . . .

"But as he which hath called you is holy, so be ye holy in all manner of conversation; because it is written, Be ye holy; for I am holy" (1 Pet. 1:15, 16).

Define holiness.

_____

_____

_____

. . . **and Knowledge**

*Read these related
Scriptures as you study
1 Corinthians 5 this week..*

Exodus 12:14–20
Matthew 18:15–20
Romans 16:17–20
1 Timothy 1:18–20

over Corinth's city limits and reached Ephesus, where Paul heard it before Chloe's household arrived. At any rate, when Paul found out about the sin, he summoned the church to take immediate disciplinary action.

No Small Matter

The sin everyone in the city of Corinth was talking about was fornication (1 Cor. 5:1). Although sexual impurity certainly wasn't foreign to pagan Corinthians, they were repulsed by the kind of immorality being practiced by a member of the Corinthian church. The offending church member was guilty of incest; he had taken his father's wife, likely his stepmother. Leviticus 18:8 specifically forbade this relationship.

Q1. Why is unsaved society appalled at times by immorality in the lives of Christians?

_____

_____

A Christian should lead a life beyond reproach, but if he sins, he should confess the sin and forsake it (1 John 1:9). The longer a Christian embraces sin and is embraced by it, the harder it seems to escape from its clutches. The sinning Corinthian Christian should have turned to the Lord for forgiveness and the power to break the illicit relationship. In turn, the Lord would have forgiven him and provided a way of escape

47

(1 Cor. 10:13). Unfortunately, the man kept on committing the sin, and his fellow church members kept on condoning it.

Take Action!

Paul rebuked the Corinthian believers because they weren't disturbed by the sin in their midst (5:2). These believers had been saved from the degradation of wicked Corinth. Many of them had practiced immorality before they were redeemed from sin. Now they were accepting flagrant immorality without so much as raising an eyebrow. It was time for action!

What did Paul suggest? Weighing all the evidence in front of him, he concluded that the offender was guilty and ought to be excommunicated from the church (vv. 3–5). He instructed the membership to do this when they gathered together in the Lord's name, with the Lord's authority undergirding their action. The sinning had brought reproach on the whole church, and it was the responsibility of the whole church to judge the offense.

Q2. Why is it so difficult to exercise church discipline?

_____

_____

_____

Q3. Read Matthew 18:15–20. Does the promise of verse 20 apply directly to every Christian gathering or just to the gathering of a church for a disciplinary purpose? Why?

_____

_____

_____

_____

The purpose of the excommunication was "the destruction of the flesh" (v. 5). Probably Paul anticipated the offender would experience some physical affliction after being removed from the church. The goal of the discipline was "that the spirit may be saved in the day of the Lord Jesus" (v. 5). In other words, while the disciplinary action would be painful, it was for the sinning member's spiritual good. This should always be the goal of church discipline; and, as 2 Corinthians 2:7 reveals, it was realized in this case.

Q4. Read Galatians 6:1. *How does this verse relate to church discipline?*

_____

_____

_____

Leaven on the Loose

The Corinthian church took pride in its broad-mindedness. It tolerated sin without raising a fuss. "Your glorying is not good," Paul charged. "Know ye not that a little leaven leaveneth the whole lump?" (v. 6). One person's sin affected the whole church. Today, too, a church's reputation and message are often judged on the basis of one member's wicked behavior.

Q5. *How does the account of Joshua 7 relate to the proverb, "A little leaven leaveneth the whole lump"?*

_____

_____

In Old Testament times every Jewish family was required to search and remove all leaven from their house in preparation for the Passover (Exod. 12:18–20; 13:6,

7). Similarly, the Corinthian believers needed to rid their spiritual house of the leaven of sin. By disciplining the offender in their midst, their church would be like a new lump of dough, free of leaven (1 Cor. 5:7a).

Positionally, all believers are pure in God's sight because Christ, the Lamb of God, was sacrificed at Calvary in order to give believers His righteousness (2 Cor. 5:21). ". . . Ye are unleavened," Paul reminded the Corinthian Christians (1 Cor. 5:7). But now the Corinthians needed to close the gap between what they were positionally in Christ and what they appeared to be in the eyes of their unsaved neighbors. So Paul exhorted, "Therefore let us keep the feast, not with old leaven, neither with the leaven of malice and wickedness; but with the unleavened bread of sincerity and truth" (v. 8). Pure motives and a life of integrity always serve as strong supporting evidence for the gospel.

A Family Matter

Sometimes parents caution their children not to run with the wrong crowd. The rationale is that bad kids can lead good kids into trouble. This well-known admonition can be modified slightly to apply to Christians of all ages. We need to watch our social life. Paul put it this way: "I wrote unto you in an epistle not to company with fornicators" (v. 9). According to Paul, social mixing with violaters of normal sexual behavior as defined by Scripture is forbidden. In verse 11, he broadened this prohibition to include the covetous, anyone greedy of gain and quick to take advantage of others; the idolater, who worships another god; the railer, one who abuses others; the drunkard; and the extortioner, who seizes more than is rightfully his.

Paul told the Corinthians not to eat with those who fell into any of the categories he listed in verse 11. This injunction called upon the Christians to abstain from inviting an immoral brother or sister home for a meal and from accepting a similar invitation from that person. Likely, this injunction also included the communion table. If an offending Christian was allowed to socialize with fellow believers on a fellowship-as-usual basis, he would assume everyone condoned his sin and would see no reason to abandon it.

The injunction did not apply outside the church. As Paul indicated, a Christian would have to "go out of the world" (v. 10) to avoid social contact with immoral, unsaved people. Besides, the church is responsible only for disciplining its own members; God will judge the unsaved (vv. 12, 13).

Q6. What actions can a Christian take to avoid being influenced by immoral speech and conduct so prevalent in society?

_____

_____

_____

Time for Action

• The way you live affects not only your testimony but also the testimony of your church. Do areas in your life need a spiritual checkup and recuperation? If so, how will you correct what is wrong?

• Does a Christian overtaken in a fault need your concern and counsel? What will you do to help restore him or her to good spiritual health?

• Do you work with someone whose lifestyle is immoral? How can you witness effectively to that person?

• Isolation from the world isn't in God's plan for Christians, but insulation from the world's evil influences is in His plan (John 17:15, 18). What will you do to cooperate with this plan?

6 Family Matters

† 1 Corinthians 6

*Believers should reflect Christian character
in their Christian family relationships and
in their personal conduct.*

Picture the scene: Custodian H and Trustee W are in court. Both are Christians and members of Loving Fellowship Baptist Church of Notown, U.S.A. Custodian H's attorney is alongside him, and the church's attorney is alongside Trustee W. Custodian H is suing the church for $10,000.

Here's what led to this court case. Loving Fellowship Baptist Church hired Mr. H to be the church custodian, giving him a one-year contract, signed by Mr. W and the other church trustees. After a month and a half, the trustees fired Custodian H, alleging that he failed to provide adequate custodial service. They specifically mentioned scrunched-up bulletins in the pew racks, unsanitary restrooms, window smears and dust on the communion table. When they fired him, they gave him one week's severance pay. But Custodian H charges he had a one-year contract and therefore has a right to one-year's pay. He is suing Loving Fellowship Baptist Church for 47 weeks' pay.

A farfetched situation? Not really. Lawsuits involving Christians are becoming more frequent these days, and they are never pleasant. How necessary are such lawsuits? Can Christians resolve their differences outside the courtroom? First Corinthians 6 offers a helpful approach to this thorny problem.

Q1. Do you feel lawsuits involving Christians damage their testimony in the eyes of attorneys and judges? Why or why not?

_____

_____

_____

Greek cities in the first century brimmed with lawsuits. The courts seemed to serve as entertainment centers for the many people who enjoyed a spirited legal contest. People's basic interests haven't changed through the centuries, and today many homes turn their attention to TV courtroom dramas—both real-life and fictional. In first-century Athens there were private arbitrators, court-appointed public arbitrators (all citizens in their 60th year had to serve as arbitrators) and juries as large as 6,000 citizens. Legal matters in a city like Athens or Corinth seeped into the Greek mind

---

Grow in Grace . . .

"Do ye not know that the saints shall judge the world? and if the world shall be judged by you, are ye unworthy to judge the smallest matters?" (1 Cor. 6:2).

saints: Christians, all who are set apart unto God

shall judge the world: see 2 Timothy 2:12a

Does our everyday conduct match our credentials? Meditate on this verse this week.

. . . **and Knowledge**

Read these related
Scriptures as you study
1 Corinthians 6 *this week.*

Romans 12:10–21
1 Corinthians 10:23–33
2 Peter 2:8–14
Revelation 2:24–29

and filtered into the very being of a Greek citizen. Legal issues, including lawsuits, were in their blood!

Keep It in the Family!

Unfortunately, the tendency to sue for the slightest reason lingered with Corinthians who had become Christians. Primed for legal battle, Christians dragged one another before unsaved judges. They preferred to settle their differences in a legal setting instead of a family setting—in court instead of in church (1 Cor. 6:1). The apostle Paul rebuked them for doing this and encouraged them to resolve their differences by seeking counsel within the church family.

Q2. What spiritual gifts are helpful in resolving differences among Christians?

_____

_____

Differences among Christians occur in spite of our oneness in Christ. We may not be able to avoid them, but we can avoid their destructiveness. Instead of letting differences shred our fellowship, we can agree to disagree agreeably. We can relate to one another in a courteous and loving manner. We can forgive and forge ahead in the Lord's work with our hearts joined together (1 Cor. 13:1, 5; Phil. 4:1–4).

By dragging one another into court, the Corinthian Christians once again displayed their carnality. A re-

55

taliatory spirit emanates from a carnal disposition; a loving and forgiving spirit emanates from a disposition controlled by the Holy Spirit. Referring to the Savior, in Whose steps we are to walk, Peter wrote: "Who, when he was reviled, reviled not again; when he suffered, he threatened not; but committed himself to him that judgeth righteously" (1 Pet. 2:23). If we were more like the Savior, we would be more concerned about displaying righteousness than demanding rights!

W. Wilbur Welch writes about a pastor who unintentionally said something that angered a deacon. The deacon led him to the door, pushed him out of the house and shut the door in his face. As the pastor walked to his car, he felt indignant and resentful. Then he realized these unwholesome emotions had replaced the joy of the Lord. Returning to the deacon's door, he humbly asked the deacon to forgive him. The apology brought a warm response, and the two men were reconciled to each other. The pastor had set a good example by determining to do what was right instead of determining to get even!

Q3. Read James 3:13–18. *How does this passage relate to the subject of differences among Christians?*

_____

_____

_____

Paul used a series of questions in 1 Corinthians 6:2 and 3 to confront the Corinthian church. He designed these to show the Corinthian church how foolish it was not to take care of its own problems.

"Do ye not know that the saints shall judge the world?" Paul asked (v. 2). This judging will occur when

Jesus Christ returns with His raptured saints to rule our planet (Dan. 7:22; Matt. 19:28; Luke 22:30; Rev. 20:1–6).

"Know ye not that we shall judge angels," Paul inquired (v. 3). Second Peter 2:4 and Jude 6 refer to the final judgment of fallen angels. Somehow Christians will participate in this judgment, although the Scriptures do not give any details.

Tying all this together, Paul asked why the Corinthians couldn't settle their own disputes. If they had been spiritual, even the least wise members in their fellowship could have cemented the fractured relationships without help from an unsaved court (v. 4). The Corinthian church should have been ashamed that its members hauled one another into court instead of turning to an arbitrator in the church (vv. 5–7a).

Absorb the Hurt

Paul asked the Corinthians why they were unwilling to suffer wrong instead of pushing offending brothers into court (v. 7b). There is no gain in getting one's own way at the expense of one's testimony. Too much is lost to call a favorable court decision a gain!

By advocating a policy of no retaliation, Paul didn't put his seal of approval on the sin of defrauding (robbing) a brother. In verse 8 he denounced it. Both the act of defrauding a brother and the reaction of taking the guilty brother to court were wrong. Both clashed with the kind of character God wanted the believers at Corinth to display. He wanted them to display righteousness. Surely, righteous people ought to be able to resolve their differences without having to go to court.

All the Corinthian Christians had been saved from sin, but some of them had been saved from the worst dregs of sin (vv. 9–11a). How would it look if these "washed," "sanctified" and "justified" believers dragged one another before unsaved judges? Wouldn't their testimony fall flat if they couldn't find an arbitrator in the church? By taking legal action, wouldn't they be announcing that Christianity couldn't solve their problems?

Free to Be Different

If the Corinthian Christians believed it didn't matter how they acted, they were badly mistaken. God hadn't saved them just so they could be forgiven; He saved them so they could be Christlike. They had been liberated *from* sin, not liberated *to* sin. Paul encouraged them to lead disciplined lives in constant recognition of Christ's ownership of them.

"All things are lawful unto me," Paul explained in verse 12, "but all things are not expedient [profitable]: all things are lawful for me, but I will not be brought under the power of any." Some things are not profitable either for the doer or the receiver. If an action hurts another person, the doer is at fault. Someone has observed, "I can walk down a street and swing my right arm as much as I please; but my liberty ends where your nose begins." Similarly, a Christian should ask if his action will injure someone else. If the answer is yes, he should forego the action.

Plato taught that a free man has the power to choose slavery; but once he has chosen slavery, he no longer has the power to choose freedom. Christian liberty functions like this. It is wrong to exercise your liberty if, by exercising it, you lose your power of self-control. Whatever makes you a slave is wrong.

Continuing his argument that Christians ought to behave differently from unsaved people, Paul discussed the importance of controlling physical appetites. Although we must eat to live, we shouldn't live to eat. It is also true that other physical appetites, including a sexual appetite, serve a purpose. Nevertheless, biological processes will end when God calls us home to Heaven (v. 13). Of course, we can anticipate a resurrection (v. 14), but our resurrected bodies will not maintain biological processes.

Walking Temples

Sexual vices stamped Corinth as an especially immoral city. Corinthians worshiped numerous false deities, and sexual sin accompanied much of this worship. More than one thousand prostitutes served in the temple of Aphrodite, the goddess of love. Truly, Christians had an opportunity to offer Corinth a clear picture of God's holiness and His power to transform sinners into righteous saints. If they committed immoral acts, they would destroy the picture.

Paul told the Corinthian believers their bodies belonged to Christ. If a Christian engaged in sexual sin with a harlot, he became one flesh with her. It seemed almost incredible that a Christian would commit such a dastardly deed (vv. 15, 16). Since the Christian is united spiritually to Christ (v. 17) and his body belongs to the Lord, he should "flee fornication" (v. 18a).

Q4. Do you think the command to "flee fornication" has any implications for those who view R- or NC-rated movies?

_____

_____

Paul's exhortations about staying pure in an impure society are on the mark for Christians in the 90s. The entertainment media flaunt illicit sexual relationships as natural, enjoyable and even beneficial. Unless Christians counteract this anti-Biblical philosophy by saturating their minds and hearts with God's Word, they can easily fall to sexual temptation and destroy their lives and others' lives too. When a Christian commits fornication, he sins against his own body (v. 18b). In effect, he vandalizes the Lord's property!

Only a fool stays in an environment that fosters immoral thoughts and lures him into immorality. Joseph, the young man who found himself in Egypt, far from home, in Potiphar's house and alone with Potiphar's seductive wife, did the wise thing—he fled when she offered him sex (Gen. 39:12). Like Joseph, a Christian today needs to flee temptation by refusing to view immoral TV programs or movies. He may even need to flee from a real-life situation that's emotionally charged and capable of producing an immoral relationship.

In the Old Testament the temple stood as God's residence among His people. In the New Testament, however, God resides in His people. The Christian's body is the temple of the Holy Spirit (1 Cor. 6:19), and God holds the title deed to the temple (v. 19b). He purchased the Christian's body "with a price" (v. 20). The apostle Peter disclosed the price; he wrote that it was Jesus Christ's blood (1 Pet. 1:18, 19). Knowing that our bodies are God's purchased temples, we ought to be careful about where we take those temples, what we do with them, and even what we put in them.

God's people serve a noble purpose in the world. We represent the Lord, urging the lost to turn from their sin and to trust in the Savior. If the lost find us scrapping and sinning, how will they be convinced that Christ makes life significantly and wonderfully different? Let's obey the exhortations Paul wrote in Colossians 3:15 and 17: "And let the peace of God rule in your hearts, to the which also ye are called in one body; and be ye thankful. . . . And whatsoever ye do in word or deed, do all in the name of the Lord Jesus, giving thanks to God and the Father by him."

Time for Action

• Are you involved in a disagreement with another

Christian? What procedure will you follow in accordance with 1 Corinthians 6:1–8 to resolve this disagreement?

- How can you promote harmony in your church?
- What lifestyle changes will you make in view of the fact that your body is the temple of the Holy Spirit?
- What can you do to advance the cause of morality in your community?

8 Give Me Liberty— and Love

† 1 Corinthians 8—10

Genuine Christian liberty operates within the bounds of love for others and love for God.

Is it right or wrong to shoplift? Easy question, right? The Bible commands, "Thou shalt not steal." Case closed! Is it right or wrong to go to a racetrack if you don't intend to bet on a horse? This question is harder, isn't it? A Christian who was formerly a compulsive gambler might rule against track attendance, but another Christian, who just enjoys horses, might insist it's perfectly all right to attend. The issue is complicated by the fact that you can't find a command in the Bible that says, "Thou shalt not attend horse races."

The Corinthian church faced a difficult issue, and its members held different opinions about it. The issue concerned food offered to idols. Was it right or wrong for a Christian to eat food offered to idols?

This question didn't spring from one or two isolated incidents. Numerous family get-togethers, festivals, banquets and meals with neighbors included food offered to idols. In the sacrifice itself, part of the animal was placed on an altar and was consumed in flames. The rest was prepared for the ensuing feast. Leftover meat was either "doggy-bagged" and carried home by the feast's participants or turned over to butcher shops for sale to the public. It's easy to see how a Christian might find himself sitting at someone's dinner table with a platter of prime pagan pot roast in front of him.

Help, Paul!

The Corinthian church had asked for Paul's counsel about eating food offered to idols. He began his reply in 1 Corinthians 8:1: "Now as touching things offered unto idols, we know that we all have knowledge. Knowledge puffeth up, but charity edifieth." Knowledge alone wouldn't resolve the issue. Only love could resolve it to everyone's satisfaction!

Q1. What special temptations might confront someone with vast Bible knowledge?

_____

_____

Knowledge informed the Corinthian church that idol gods didn't exist, in spite of the fact that the pagan Corinthians worshiped them and offered food sacrifices to them. Knowledge allowed the Corinthian Christians to eat idol food at a public feast or in a private home. But some Christians hadn't been saved long. In their unsaved condition, they believed in idol gods and had sacrificed to them. Their consciences would not

Grow in Grace . . .

"Whether therefore ye eat, or drink, or whatsoever ye do, do all to the glory of God" (1 Cor. 10:31).

Meditate on this verse this week, and put it into practice.

. . . and Knowledge

*Read these related
Scriptures as you study
1 Corinthians 8—10 this
week.*

Exodus 17:1–7
Numbers 25
Romans 14
Galatians 5
1 John 4:7–12, 20, 21

allow them to eat idol food now that they were Christians (v. 7). Acting according to knowledge, the believers could eat the idol food, but love for their brothers with sensitive consciences would lead them to abstain from doing so (vv. 3–9).

Paul acknowledged there was no spiritual merit either in eating idol food or in abstaining from it (v. 8). What counted with God was conduct based on love (v. 3).

The Limits of Liberty

Suppose a Satan worshiper in your community became a Christian, joined your church and became a faithful member of your Sunday Bible School class. Suppose, further, your class decided to sponsor a Halloween party for the church's teens, complete with a haunted house and decorations of witches and goblins. How would you and your fellow adults react if the former Satan worshiper objected? Would you tell him his concerns were groundless, knowing the setting was not intended in any way to be satanic? Would you try to convince him that everyone but him considered the haunted house harmless entertainment? Or would you restructure the social and eliminate the Halloween theme and accompanying elements? What would Christian love lead you to do?

Jesus promised, "And ye shall know the truth, and the truth shall make you free" (John 8:32). Does this mean Christians are free to do whatever they choose to do? Paul answered this question in 1 Corinthians 8:9. The Corinthian Christians were not free to do anything that might trip a brother in his walk with the Lord. "But take heed," Paul told the Corinthian Christians, "lest by any means this liberty of yours become a stumblingblock to them that are weak." Love, then, sets the limits for liberty.

Q2. Is a believer with a legalistic approach to Christian living a weak or a strong brother? Why?

_____

_____

Enlarging upon this matter, Paul offered the following scenario. What might happen if a Christian with a weak conscience saw a fellow Christian at a feast in an idol's temple? Perhaps he would decide to participate in a similar feast, and thereby sin against his conscience (vv. 10, 11). The stronger Christian, then, would be sinning against his Christian brother and against Christ too (v. 12). Not wanting to be a stumbling block to anyone, Paul chose to forego liberty for the sake of a weaker brother's spiritual good (v. 13).

Have you set aside your Christian liberty at any time for the good of another Christian?

Paul's Example

Every true servant of God has critics. Even Paul didn't suit everyone. His critics accused him of being an impostor, and they advised others to reject his teachings on that basis. So Paul found himself in the position of defending his apostleship to the Corinthians. Ironically, Paul's defense of his teaching and ministry only served as another example of a believer choosing to set aside his liberty for the sake of love.

Paul first affirmed he had seen the risen Lord. "Am I not an apostle? am I not free? have I not seen Jesus Christ our Lord?" he asked (1 Cor. 9:1). Then he defended his apostleship by pointing out how God had used him to found the church in Corinth. "Are not ye my work in the Lord?" he asked (v. 1; see verse 2 as well).

Paul had the same liberties as other apostles: to eat and drink (v. 4), to marry (v. 5) and to receive financial support (v. 6). Furthermore, society's economic structure included paying wages to workers. A soldier wasn't expected to pay for his own travel, weaponry, food and supplies when he went to war. Vinedressers ate some of the grapes they harvested. And shepherds enjoyed milk from their flocks (v. 7). Besides, the Scriptures taught the principle of payment for work (v. 8). Quoting Deuteronomy 25:4, Paul informed the Corinthians, "Thou shalt not muzzle the mouth of the ox that treadeth out the corn" (v. 9). This principle, he told his readers, applied not only to oxen but also to him and his coworkers (v. 10). Having received spiritual benefits from Paul's ministry, the Corinthian Christians should have responded by supporting Paul generously (v. 11).

What Paul applied to the Corinthian church applies to churches today. A church ought to support its pastor well. Having received spiritual benefits from him, a church should reciprocate with a salary that frees him from undue financial concern. Although many dedicated pastors would rather preach without pay than be paid not to preach, a church must not take advantage of such dedication by offering a paltry salary when it has the resources to do better. As someone has observed, "Giving is a grace, but the lack of giving is a disgrace."

According to a certain story, a pastor asked a bank teller to cash his paycheck.

"I have only old, dirty bills," the teller lamented.

"That's okay," replied the pastor.

"But aren't you afraid of germs?" the teller asked.

"Not in the least," the pastor responded. "A germ couldn't live on my salary."

> Q3. *How might a pastor's credibility be affected by an austere lifestyle? a lavish lifestyle? Do these considerations apply to all Christians? Why or why not?*

_____

_____

_____

_____

_____

Although Paul was at liberty to request and receive funds from the church in Corinth, he voluntarily declined. He believed he would "hinder the gospel of Christ" if he made financial support an issue (v. 12). He merely reiterated the principle that God's ministers are supposed to be supported financially (vv. 13, 14), and he underscored his willingness to starve rather than take money from the Corinthians. He did not want to give anyone opportunity to accuse him of being in the ministry only for what he could get out of it (v. 15).

Lack of financial support wouldn't keep Paul from preaching. He was compelled by a divine summons to preach (vv. 16, 17). He presented the gospel without charge instead of insisting upon his right to be supported financially. He considered this practice rewarding in itself (v. 18).

Love above Liberty

Paul gave up his rights and became a servant to all because he wanted to win many lost persons to Christ

(v. 19). He attached a higher priority to love than to liberty! With a servant's heart, he became like a Jew in order to win Jews to Christ (v. 20), and he became like a Gentile in order to win Gentiles to Christ (v. 21). Even though his liberty in Christ gave him freedom to do certain things, he waived his liberty for the spiritual good of those with weak consciences and for the sake of the gospel (vv. 22, 23).

A converted Muslim caught the spirit of Paul's behavior. The following is his testimony:

> Since I've been saved, I know that keeping the various laws of my religion did not help one bit. One is not saved by keeping the law or observing the many practices. We were not allowed to eat any pork because it was said to defile us. After I was saved, I realized that this was foolish. However, you ask me why I don't eat ham or pork or bacon now. I am not under the law. I can be free. But when I return to my people, they will ask me if I have eaten any pork. If I say yes, then I've lost my opportunity to win them to Christ. For their sake, for the sake of their salvation, I am depriving myself of something perfectly permissible to eat.

Like a Well-conditioned Athlete

The Corinthians were well-acquainted with athletics. Their city hosted the Isthmian games, the second most popular sporting event in Greece. Only the Olympic games commanded more attention. Picking up on the Corinthians' interest in sports, Paul compared himself to a highly disciplined athlete in quest of the victor's crown (vv. 24, 25). He refused to abandon his quest of an eternal crown in order to indulge fleshly appetites. He made every move count (v. 26). His self-discipline would keep him from becoming "a castaway"—disqualified for Christian service (v. 27).

Q4. What kinds of disciplines strengthen a Christian in his walk with the Lord?

_____

_____

_____

Privilege and Responsibility

Paul wasn't finished with his discourse on liberty and love. The Corinthian believers needed a history lesson. They needed to learn from the experiences of the ancient Israelites in Moses' era (1 Cor. 10:6). All the Israelites shared certain privileges: all were redeemed from Egypt; all were guided by the glory cloud (vv. 1, 2); all were provided with food and drink by God (vv. 3, 4). But God sentenced that entire generation to death in the wilderness (v. 5). Faithful Joshua and Caleb were the sole survivors of that generation to enter Canaan.

Why review such a dismal chapter in Israel's history? The Israelites took their privileges for granted and ignored the accompanying responsibilities to worship and serve as God's separated people. They lusted and engaged in idolatry (vv. 6, 7). They committed fornication (v. 8). They put God to the test (v. 9), and they grumbled (v. 10).

The implication for the Corinthians was clear. They must not assume they were beyond falling into sin (v. 12). If they claimed their liberty allowed them to participate with idol worshipers in their festivals, they couldn't blame God if they succumbed to the environment and fell into sin. God helps His people avoid temptation; He doesn't entice them to do what is wrong (v. 13). The best way to approach a dangerous situation is to stay away from it. "Flee from idolatry," Paul advised the Corinthians (v. 14).

If the Corinthian Christians were truly wise, they

would heed Paul's admonition (v. 15). God's people must separate from compromising, unholy alliances. The Christians belonged to Christ and worshiped Him (vv. 16, 17). Just as the Israelites were bonded to the priests by eating what the priests had sacrificed, so the Corinthian Christians who ate idol food were bonded to those who worshiped idols (v. 18). Further, demons were behind the idol worship (vv. 19, 20). By participating in festivals where everyone ate food offered to idols, Corinthian Christians compromised their testimony and provoked the Lord (vv. 21, 22). Paul decided his conduct not on the basis of what he was free to do but on the basis of what would edify (vv. 23, 24).

Don't Ask Questions!

If a Christian purchased meat in a butcher shop or accepted a dinner invitation at a neighbor's house, he shouldn't ask if the food had been sacrificed to idols (vv. 25–27). He should simply eat it, believing that it was a provision from God. However, if someone informed him that it had been sacrificed to idols, he must not eat it for the sake of the other man's conscience (vv. 28, 29). This would avoid the mistaken impression that liberty is license to sin (vv. 29, 30).

Glorify God

A Christian ought to decide every questionable issue on the basis of what will glorify God (v. 31). He can ask, Will my participation give others a clearer concept of God and help persuade them to know Him, or will it have a negative effect on their concept of Him? Following Paul's example, a Christian will act in the best interest of others, always willing to forego his liberty in order to bring them to Christ (vv. 32, 33).

Time for Action

• List questionable activities that concern you.

- Do you have liberty to do any of them? all of them?
- How might your participation affect others?
- Apply the principle of love to each activity on your list.
- What will you do today to edify at least one person?
- What will you do today to glorify God?

9 The Church at Worship

† 1 Corinthians 11

True worship involves obedience to the Word and love for the Lord.

Have you seen the bumper sticker or poster announcing, "The best man for the job is a woman"? Clever wording! As a matter of fact, in many situations a woman may be the best person for the job. Many women in today's job market are certainly intelligent, knowledgeable, highly skilled and successful workers. It isn't uncommon to find women in company ownership, administration, management and supervision, and functioning there with proven expertise. Even in some churches there is the feeling that "the best pastor for the job is a woman." Indeed, in some religious circles the advisability of ordaining women has become a theological watershed. As in all things, we ought to expose this issue to the light of Scripture.

Order in the Church!

In 1 Corinthians 11 Paul addressed the issue of female leadership in the local church. First, though, he exhorted the Corinthian church to follow him, as he was following the Lord (v. 1). Then he commended the church for holding the teachings he had imparted to it (v. 2). Correction is always more palatable when preceded by a spoonful of commendation! Paul didn't state the problem that commanded his attention in 1 Corinthians 11:1–16. Apparently, it was so well-known to the Corinthians that he simply plunged in to correct it.

"The head of every man is Christ," Paul asserted in verse 3; "and the head of the woman is the man; and the head of Christ is God." Man was supposed to exercise headship over God's creation (Gen. 1:28), but he abdicated his rule when he rebelled against God and fell into sin. In Christ, however, spiritual headship is regained. The Christian man is charged with leadership under Christ.

Q1. Do you think the principle of male headship applies to the workplace? Why or why not?

_____

_____

_____

_____

Grow in Grace . . .

"Let the words of my mouth, and the meditation of my heart, be acceptable in thy sight, O LORD, my strength, and my redeemer" (Ps. 19:14).

As you worship God this week, think about the words you sing, the prayers you offer and the reflections of your heart. Are they suitable? Are they Scriptural? Are they spiritual? Worship God as your sovereign ("LORD"), your sustainer ("strength") and your Savior ("redeemer").

. . . and Knowledge

*Read these related
Scriptures as you study
1 Corinthians 11 this week.*

Matthew 26:26–30
Acts 2:41–47
1 Timothy 2
1 Peter 3:1–7

How does Paul's teaching in Galatians 3:28 fit this picture of male headship? In Christ, men and women share equal status. Both enjoy a favorable standing in God's sight. Both enjoy eternal salvation. Both have access to the throne of grace. Both enjoy membership in the family of God. Both are indwelled by the Holy Spirit. However, in church and family life, their roles and responsibilities differ by God's design. The Christian man is to fulfill a divinely appointed leadership role; the Christian woman, a subordinate and supportive role. By no means, though, is the woman a passive observer in either the church or home. Many demands on her time in both spheres of ministry can set a pace for her that might exhaust the average man. One thing is clear: Scripture does not equate subordination with slavery nor headship with dictatorship.

Proof that subordination does not imply inferiority lies in the fact that Christ subordinated Himself to the Father, though He and the Father are coequal, coeternal and co-essential. "The head of Christ is God," 1 Corinthians 11:3 proclaims. Also, it is important to note that male headship ranks under Christ: "The head of every man is Christ" (v. 3). If a man honors Christ, a woman will most likely welcome his leadership.

Order on Display

Paul instructed the men in the Corinthian church to uncover their heads when they prayed or prophesied. For a man not to do so was to dishonor his head (v. 4).

85

If he covered his head, he would give the impression that he disclaimed his divinely appointed headship. It would also suggest he denied Christ His headship over him.

The women in the Corinthian church were to cover their heads when they prayed or prophesied (v. 5). This would show their acceptance of divinely appointed headship and also their regard for modesty. Only immoral, insubordinate women went about in public with their heads uncovered. Some have suggested that Corinthian prostitutes and adulteresses may have had their heads shaved. Paul wrote that a Christian woman who refused to cover her head might as well shave her head. If she feared the reputation that would bring, she should wear a head covering (v. 6).

> Q2. *What cultural considerations, if any, do Christians in North America observe in their church services?*

_____

_____

_____

Since man was created as "the image and glory of God" (v. 7a), he should not cover his head when praying or prophesying. On the other hand, because "the woman is the glory of the man" (v. 7b) and was created from him and for him (vv. 8, 9), she should cover her head. Even the angels expect to see women comply with the divinely established male/female order (v. 10). Angels understand the importance of accepting God's appointed order and rank. When some of their number refused to accept the position God had assigned to them, they fell!

Some in Corinth might have thought Paul's comments meant woman is inferior to man, so the apostle reminded his readers in verses 11 and 12 that the well-being of each is dependent upon the other. Man and woman share equality and mutual dependency.

Even good sense taught the man to uncover his head at worship and the woman to cover her head. It was normal for a woman to have longer hair than a man. Her hair was her glory and covering (vv. 13–15). It should have taught her that God wanted her to cover her head at worship.

If anyone contested Paul's teaching on this subject, that one would stand alone, because no other church followed practices that ignored male headship (v. 16).

Although social customs have changed through the centuries, God's principle of male headship continues. Out of love for the Lord and in obedience to His Word, Christian women will honor this principle. They will not cast aside the symbols of female modesty or their responsibility to rank under the man in leadership.

Order at the Lord's Table

Next, Paul addressed another problem of the Corinthian assembly. The communion service (also called the Lord's Supper, the Lord's Table or the Table of the Lord) gives believers an opportunity to reflect upon Christ's redemptive work at Calvary and their relationship to Him. Paul wasted no time in rebuking the Corinthians for their abuses of the Lord's Supper (v. 17). They had turned a spiritually rich observance into a divisive event (v. 18). By contrast, the bad conduct of some highlighted the spiritual character of others (v. 19).

Specifically, the bad conduct included not only divisiveness but also overindulgence and drunkenness. The well-to-do Corinthians brought food for a feast that preceded communion; but instead of sharing it with their poor brethren, they pounced on it before the poor had so much as a chance to smell the aroma

(vv. 20, 21). If they wanted to stuff their bellies and drown their thirst, they should have stayed home (v. 22). Obviously, the offenders had carried pagan festival manners to church, but they should have left them behind when they trusted in Christ as Savior.

The word "communion" suggests a sharing together, a joint-participation. When believers gather together in the local church for the Lord's Supper, their hearts and minds should be linked together in mutual love for the Lord and for one another. Grudges and prejudices are totally out of character with the New Testament's family concept of God's redeemed people. How can any Christian retain a proud spirit or an unforgiving spirit in view of the fact that Jesus Christ humbled Himself, even unto death, and forgave rebellious sinners who turned to Him as Savior? Since He has showered His love and grace on us, how dare we harbor bitterness toward any who partake of the Lord's Supper with us!

> Q3. *How does the Lord's Supper relate to social barriers that may exist in a local church?*

_____

_____

_____

In one church where I served as pastor, I was about to give the trays of communion bread to the deacons to distribute to the congregation when a visitor asked permission to speak. Knowing this man was a Christian and a member of a church of like faith, I gave the permission he requested. He told the congregation he was absent from his own church because he was out of fellowship with his pastor. He confessed that his attitude toward his pastor was sinful. He announced his intention to ask his pastor's forgiveness and be restored to the fellowship of his own church. Such sensitivity to communion's focus on believers' bonds in Christ is an important part of any observance of the ordinance.

Orderly Observance

Paul received his information about the Lord's Supper directly from the Lord and passed it along to the Corinthian church (v. 23a). He explained the Lord instituted the ordinance the night He was betrayed. He took bread, gave thanks, broke it and gave it to His disciples to eat in remembrance of Him (vv. 23a, 24). Then, "after the same manner," the Lord took the cup. He revealed that it signified the new covenant in His blood, and He commanded His disciples to drink the cup in remembrance of Him (v. 25). Paul assured the Corinthian believers that every time they observed the Lord's Supper they proclaimed "the Lord's death till he come" (v. 26).

The Lord's Supper does not convey saving merit to those who partake of the ordinance. Salvation comes only by the grace of God (Eph. 2:8, 9). It is not based on what we do at communion but on what Christ did for us at Calvary (Rom. 3:24). In communion, believers remember the Savior's crucifixion and anticipate His coming. Communion is not a display of the participants' religious worth; it is a picture of the Savior's redemptive work!

Since the Lord's Supper conveys a message of great spiritual significance, no one should approach the Table of the Lord "unworthily" (1 Cor. 11:27). Of course, none of us are worthy of Christ's sacrifice at Calvary. He died for us when we were rebellious, ungodly, Hell-deserving sinners (Rom. 5:6–10). Our only worth is what we are in Christ. Paul's reference to partaking communion "unworthily" reflected the Corinthians' irreverent and divisive conduct at the communion service. Their cliquishness and carnal feasting were totally out of line with the somber truth that Christ's body was nailed to the cross and His blood was shed for them (1 Cor. 11:27).

Self-examination should precede our partaking of the Lord's Supper (v. 28). Attitudes such as pride, bitterness, indifference, hatred, grudge-bearing and disobedience should be confessed and forsaken. Flippancy and daydreaming insult the character of the service. Reverence, remembrance and rededication suit the occasion.

Paul cautioned the Corinthians that the Lord would chasten anyone who partook of the Lord's Supper with a sinful attitude (v. 29). He had already stretched His chastening hand over the congregation. Many members were sick, and many had died as a result of their unholy approach to communion (v. 30). If they had inspected their attitudes and actions and corrected them, they would have avoided such chastening (v. 31). Nevertheless, in chastening them, the Lord distinguished them from the unsaved, who will be consigned to eternal punishment and separation from Him (v. 32).

Q4. Is sickness always an evidence of divine chastisement? Why or why not?

_____

_____

Having pointed out the sinfulness of the Corinthians' behavior at the communion service, the significance of the ordinance and the solemnity of God's chastening, Paul urged his readers to correct their disorderly behavior (v. 33). If anyone regarded the Lord's Supper as an opportunity to satisfy his appetite, he was well-advised to eat at home rather than risk God's disciplinary action (v. 34).

If our worship is to honor God, we must follow His prescribed order and approach Him humbly, reverently and with cleansed hearts and minds. Our Lord,

Who gave His all for us, deserves such worship and all that we are and have.

Time for Action

• How can you honor God in the role (leadership/support) He has given to you?

• Examine your attitude toward fellow Christians. If you harbor any ill will, confess it and forsake it.

• Write a brief poem or paragraph expressing your thanks to the Lord for His sacrifice at Calvary.

• Share the good news of salvation with someone this week.

10 You Are Gifted

† 1 Corinthians 12; 13

The Christian ought to use his spiritual gifts in love.

The Lord has charged believers with the task of carrying out the Great Commission. The responsibility is staggering, but our Lord's enabling is sufficient. Whatever His will dictates, His grace delivers. As a matter of fact, God has gifted every believer—including you—with special abilities to accomplish His will.

> *Q1. What is the difference between a natural talent and a spiritual gift?*

_____

_____

_____

Gifts for Everybody!

In a letter to Paul, the Corinthians had asked for information about spiritual gifts (1 Cor. 12:1a). Although they didn't lack any gifts (v. 7), they didn't understand how spiritual gifts were distributed or how they were supposed to be used. As a result, the Corinthian Christians were coveting the most visible and spectacular gifts instead of cooperating in using their gifts for the work of the ministry. Paul didn't want this display of ignorance to continue (v. 1b).

Like the Christians at Corinth, some believers today may not realize God has endowed them with spiritual gifts. They may assume they have no ability—nothing—to dedicate to Christian service. "If only I had the ability to teach or preach," they lament, "I would do so gladly. But I can't do anything for the Lord; I have absolutely no talent for anything." In 1 Corinthians 12 and 13 Paul delivers strong encouragement for them and for all who want to use their spiritual gifts effectively.

What a difference God had made in the Corinthians' lives! He had lifted them out of slavish devotion to lifeless idols and had placed them under the command of the living Lord Jesus (vv. 2, 3). Although some false teachers, who called themselves spiritual, called Jesus "accursed," the Spirit of God had led the Corinthians to the truth about Jesus—He is "the Lord" (v. 3).

As Lord, Jesus Christ had the right to direct the Corinthian church. Its members should have submit-

Grow in Grace . . .

"And now abideth faith, hope, charity, these three; but the greatest of these is charity" (1 Cor. 13:13).

Faith accepts the promises of God.
Hope anticipates the fulfillment of the promises of God.
Love cherishes the God of the promises.

Tell God you love Him.
Show that you love Him.

. . . and Knowledge

Read these related Scriptures as you study 1 Corinthians 12 and 13.

Exodus 31:1–6
John 13:1–15, 34, 35
Romans 12:3–16
Ephesians 4:7–16
1 Peter 4:8–11

ted themselves to Him and been willing to trust Him to bestow abilities for ministry as He deemed best. Paul assured them spiritual gifts come in a variety of forms, with different functions and results, but the triune God determines all of these (vv. 4–6). The fact is, no Corinthian Christian was overlooked in the divine distribution of gifts, and no Christian is overlooked today either. Paul declared: "The manifestation of the Spirit is given to every man to profit withal . . . . But all these worketh that one and selfsame Spirit, dividing to every man severally as he will" (vv. 7, 11).

Q2. How does the subject of Christian stewardship relate to spiritual gifts?

_____

_____

_____

First-Century Gifts and Twentieth-Century Gifts

Some of the gifts the Holy Spirit imparted to the church in the first century aren't available to twentieth-century Christians. Why? Because we don't need them. They served a purpose, then faded away when they weren't needed any longer. This doesn't mean they weren't beneficial; it simply means they were replaced with something better.

95

Although some Bible teachers believe several of the gifts Paul identified in verses 8–10 are given today, it seems best to assign all of them to the first century. They were special gifts imparted to first-century Christians before the writing of the New Testament was completed. Listed in order, they are the word of wisdom, the word of knowledge, faith, healing, miracles, prophecy, discerning of spirits, tongues and the interpretation of tongues.

When the New Testament became available in written form, it provided the wisdom and knowledge the Church needed for understanding and applying God's will to various kinds of situations. It also provided the basis for faith (Rom. 10:17). We believe God because His Word teaches us to believe Him. Healing, miracles, tongues and the interpretation of tongues fizzled out when the New Testament became available. Whereas these special gifts authenticated the Christian message, the New Testament became the authenticator. Anyone who wants to know whether a message is authentic may compare it to the message of the New Testament. If it differs, it is false; if it agrees, it is true. On this basis, the gift of discerning of spirits ceased. The New Testament shows whether a teaching is true or false.

It seems that some of these gifts had already disappeared by the time Hebrews was written. Hebrews 2:3 and 4 describe such gifts as signs that had accompanied the apostles' preaching.

First Corinthians 12:28–30 also identifies these first-century temporary gifts and adds the following: apostles, prophets, teachers, helps and governments. Apostles and prophets contributed to the founding of the church (Eph. 2:20), but later their offices faded away. The apostles were directly commissioned by the Lord. They witnessed His resurrection. And they received miraculous powers from Him that authenticated their preaching (Heb. 2:3, 4). By direct revelation the prophets spoke forth a word from God and foretold the future (Acts 11:27, 28; 19:6).

The gifts of teachers, helps and governments apply to ministry today. Teachers help others understand and apply the Scriptures. Christians who assist those in need may be said to have the gift of helps. The gift of governments likely refers to the ability to administer in a local church. The word "governments" comes from a Greek word that describes a pilot of a ship who steers the vessel through difficult waters to a safe harbor. No doubt, those who serve wisely on committees in the local church have this spiritual gift.

Twentieth-century Christians may have other gifts also. Romans 12:7 and 8 list the gifts of ministry (service), teaching, exhortation (encouragement and admonition to grow spiritually and to serve the Lord), giving (in uncommon measure), ruling (presiding over a congregation) and mercy (kindness, considerateness, helpfulness). Ephesians 4:11 adds the gifts of evangelists and pastors to our list of permanent gifts available to twentieth-century Christians.

Teamwork

A professing Christian in the West, formerly a member of Lebanon's Olympic volleyball team, occasionally challenges amateur volleyball teams to compete against him. Single-handedly he gives each competing team all it can handle. Obviously, spectators are impressed with his skill and wonder what he might accomplish with equally skilled teammates.

The apostle Paul compared spiritually gifted Christians to members of the human body (1 Cor. 12:12–27). The smooth functioning of the human body testifies to the value of teamwork. The foot, hand, ears, nose, eyes and all the other parts of the body work in harmony with one another under the direction of the head. The brain sends signals to body parts, and those parts respond cooperatively as commanded. The foot must not feel it isn't part of the body because it isn't a hand, and an ear must not feel slighted because it isn't an eye. Every part of the body plays a significant role for the good of the entire body.

The spinal canal is anything but a glamorous part of the body, but it plays an extremely important role in the general good health and activity of the whole body. Until I had back trouble a few years ago, I really hadn't spent much time thinking about my spinal canal. As a matter of fact, the Panama Canal and the Suez Canal commanded more of my attention. Even the Welland Canal that joins Lake Erie and Lake Ontario had captured my attention from time to time, because I grew up in a city traversed by the Welland Canal. But one day my spinal canal commanded a major share of my attention.

"Your back trouble is due in part to herniated disks and spinal stynosis," the neurosurgeon told me.

"What is spinal stynosis?" I asked. It sounded like Greek to me, and it sounded bad.

It was.

The surgeon explained it was a narrowing of the spinal canal, a birth defect in my case, which was impinging on the spinal cord and causing numbness, muscle atrophe and pain in the right leg. "If we don't get you into surgery soon, you'll be paralyzed," he announced.

A few days later, the surgeon repaired the herniated disks and widened the spinal canal. Suddenly, my spinal canal had leaped from obscurity in my thinking to prominence. Even the Panama and Suez canals seemed relatively unimportant by comparison.

Every part of the human body, seen or unseen, is important. So is every member of the body of Christ!

When you became a Christian, the Holy Spirit baptized you (placed you) into the body of Christ (1 Cor.

12:13). Furthermore, He gave you at least one spiritual gift so you would be an essential contributor to the spiritual vitality and service of the entire body. You may not be as visible as the pastor in your service role, but you are just as essential. What might happen if every member of your church employed his or her spiritual gifts humbly, lovingly, faithfully and cooperatively, in obedience to the Head of the Church? What impact would that teamwork make on your community? It is possible the impact might be felt not only at home but also a continent or two away!

> Q3. Why is union with Christ basic to the employment of spiritual gifts?

_____

_____

The Greatest Gift Is Love

In 1 Corinthians 12:22–26 Paul campaigned for mutual respect and caring among Christians. A team that lacks mutual respect and concern for its members may have a losing season regardless of how much outstanding talent it has. A winning team believes each team member is vitally important.

If a local church cherishes the Truth—God's Word—it has the message people desperately need. If it has genuine love, too, it has the ministry people desperately need. Message and ministry complement each other. Jesus not only communicated God's love for sinners, He also demonstrated God's love for sinners. He told people about God's love, and He touched their lives with that love.

The Corinthians didn't care about others; they just cared about the gifts they wanted for themselves. Paul told them in 1 Corinthians 12:31 they were coveting the best gifts ("covet" in verse 31 may be translated, "you are coveting"), but he would show them "a more excellent way." That more excellent way is mapped out in chapter 13 as the way of love!

If a church building was so cold that frost formed on the inside of the windows, what could be done to remove the frost? The members could scrape the frost from the windows and shiver while they scraped. Or the church could light a fire in the furnace and watch the frost melt away. A church is never cold to the Lord or to others if love's warmth permeates its fellowship.

Whatever a Christian's spiritual gift is, he should exercise it in love—selfless, sacrificial love. Even the most eloquent oration delivered without love merely gongs and clashes as far as God is concerned (1 Cor. 13:1). And gifts such as prophecy, wisdom, knowledge, faith and giving fall flat unless they are exercised in love (vv. 2, 3). Ministry only excels and endures if it is rendered in love.

A loving Christian puts up with a lot and reciprocates with kindness. He doesn't envy someone else's possessions, talents or situation. He doesn't promote himself or develop a big head (v. 4). Love compels him to put the Lord first, others second and himself last.

A loving Christian is well-mannered. He doesn't push himself forward at others' expense. He doesn't carry a chip on his shoulder or a grudge in his heart (v. 5).

A Christian who loves the God of the Word, the Word of God and the people of God doesn't find any delight in evil. He delights in the truth (v. 6).

Love in a Christian's heart enables him to keep confidences, be confident, look confidently to the future and be an overcomer (v. 7).

Some so-called ministries rise like rockets and fall like rocks because they are motivated by pride instead of love. Love will outlast prophecies, tongues and knowledge, Paul advised the Corinthians (v. 8). He understood that his knowledge and prophesying were incomplete (v. 9). Christians at Corinth didn't know everything about spiritual matters; nor could they foretell or tell forth everything. But someday the "perfect" would arrive. There would be no further need of incomplete knowledge and prophesying. Just as maturity changes the way a person thinks and acts, making childhood's ways obsolete, so the arrival of the "perfect" would render partial knowledge and prophesying obsolete (vv. 10, 11). At that time, Christians will see "face to face" (v. 12)

What is the "perfect"? Since prophesying resumes in the Tribulation (Joel 2:28; Rev. 11:3), it doesn't seem to refer to the completion of the New Testament or to the Rapture. The most plausible interpretation suggests the eternal state. When a believer enters the presence of the Lord, either by death or the Rapture, he becomes fully Christlike (1 John 3:2). Then, all partial knowledge and proclamations about God's truth will be past; a face to face meeting with the Lord will provide perfect knowledge and a perfect declaration about Him and our eternal Home.

Faith, hope and love are excellent qualities (1 Cor. 13:13). Faith accepts God's Word. Hope anticipates the ultimate fulfillment of God's Word. But love is the greatest quality. Faith will not be necessary in Heaven. Hope will have been satisfied when we enter Heaven. But love is eternal. Throughout eternity, we shall express our love to God for all that He is and for all that He has done for us. And we shall live in an environment where the central Person is Christ, Who loved us and gave Himself for us (Gal. 2:20).

God has gifted you for service. In return, give Him a servant's heart of love that spills over to others!

Time for Action

• What spiritual gifts do you feel God has given you?

• Ask Christian friends who are well-acquainted with you to tell what spiritual gifts they believe you have.

• Are you using your spiritual gifts? How might you start using them or developing them further?

• Do you show love in your Christian service? What can you do this week in a spirit of Christian love?

11 Tongues Talk

† 1 Corinthians 14

A church should declare God's truth in understandable words and in an orderly manner.

It happens in most families at Christmas. Each child gets presents, but one present seems to capture not only the recipient's interest but the other kids' interest too. It may be a less expensive gift than the others, and it may not be very durable; yet everyone wants it, and the other gifts pale in comparison. The resulting confusion is more than a little stressful to the whole family.

> Q1. *What spiritual gift do you believe charismatic churches emphasize above the rest?*

_____

God had blessed the Christian family at Corinth with an abundance of spiritual gifts, each distributed by the Holy Spirit to benefit the recipient's ministry. Unfortunately, the Corinthians seemed to focus their interest on a few gifts to the neglect of the others. The gift of tongues, in particular, captured their interest, and this threw the whole family into confusion and disorder. Even the worship service became unruly and sensuous instead of orderly and spiritual. The situation drew a challenging response from Paul.

The Priority of Prophesying

Having just emphasized love as God's greatest gift, Paul urged the Corinthians to pursue love (1 Cor. 14:1a). He encouraged them to desire spiritual gifts for ministry but to understand the priority of prophesying (v. 1b).

Paul rated the prophetic ministry highly because it included the proclaiming of truths not yet written or compiled into the New Testament. Interestingly, unlike so many experience-seeking Christians, Paul didn't rate tongues highly. Those who regard speaking in tongues as the Cadillac among the spiritual gifts ought to consider carefully the following observations:

1. The gift of tongues doesn't occupy a prominent place in any New Testament listing of spiritual gifts.

2. Speaking in an unknown tongue is never identified as a sign of being filled with the Spirit.

3. "Unknown" in "unknown tongue" (vv. 2, 4, 13, 14, 19, 27) was added by the translators; it isn't in the Greek text.

4. Speaking in tongues was a sign to unbelievers, not to believers (v. 22).

5. The Christians at Corinth were spiritually immature. Their clamoring for the gift of tongues underscored this immaturity.

6. The Corinthians' speaking in tongues contributed

Grow in Grace . . .

"For God is not the author of confusion, but of peace, as in all churches of the saints" (1 Cor. 14:33).

Memorize and meditate upon this verse this week.

. . . and Knowledge

*Read these related
Scriptures as you study
1 Corinthians 14 this week.*

Isaiah 28:9–13
Acts 2:1–21
Acts 10:34–48
Acts 20:17–28
2 Timothy 4:1–8

to confusion and disorder in worship, whereas "God is not the author of confusion" (v. 33).

If someone in the Corinthian church spoke in a language no one understood, he might declare wonderful spiritual truths, but no one would profit from it. Only God would understand what the speaker said (v. 2), and only the speaker would benefit spiritually (v. 4a). On the other hand, if someone prophesied and thereby declared spiritual truths, others would be edified, exhorted and comforted (vv. 3, 4).

Paul didn't oppose the use of the gift of tongues, if it was done properly. If the Corinthians employed the gift, someone had to interpret the tongue (language); otherwise no one would be edified. As far as Paul was concerned, the church would gain far more if someone prophesied (v. 5). If he visited Corinth, he preferred to arrive with a direct disclosure about spiritual truth, or with knowledge of such truth, or with a declaration of truth, or with teaching about truth (v. 6).

Q2. What would be an appropriate response today to someone who claimed to be a prophet with a new revelation from God?

_____

_____

Flute, Harp and Trumpet

Most adults enjoy music they can sing along with,

105

or at least accompany by whistling or humming. They enjoy music that conveys joy or brings back fond memories or lightens the burdens of the day. Of course, Christian adults especially appreciate good inspirational music. Occasionally we catch the disruptive, discordant and even decadent booming, banging and bashing volume of what some individuals call music when a motorist with wide-open windows pulls alongside our car at a red traffic light. I used to say such music was for the birds, but out of respect for birds I stopped saying it!

Paul compared speaking in tongues without an interpreter to instrumental sounds without pitch and rhythm. If a flute or stringed instrument disregarded orderly composition, a listener wouldn't know how to respond (v. 7). Further, Paul compared speaking in tongues without an interpreter to a military trumpet blast that didn't signal anything and therefore served no purpose as far as the troops were concerned (v. 8). Unless the Corinthians spoke in a familiar language, they might as well speak into the air (v. 9).

Every language has meaning, Paul told his readers (v. 10), but if two persons spoke to each other in unfamiliar languages, they would be foreigners to each other (v. 11). Paul wanted the Corinthian believers to channel their zeal for spiritual gifts in the right direction by edifying one another (v. 12).

Language study is one of the most difficult phases of missionary life, but it is also one of the most necessary. A missionary must stretch his memory, exercise his brain and at times contort his tongue in order to converse in the language of his mission field. He struggles through language school and subjects himself to the laughter of nationals when he tries to converse in his newly acquired language. Why does he stick with it? Because he wants to share the gospel with the people to whom God has sent him. He knows they must understand his message in order to respond in faith to Christ. In Corinth, too, no one would respond to a message delivered in a worship service unless he understood the language in which the message was communicated. If someone spoke in an unfamiliar language, he needed an interpreter (v. 13).

Q3. Why is Bible translation such an important ministry?

_____

_____

_____

According to verses 14–17, even prayer and praise required an intelligent understanding on the part of the hearers. Paul himself spoke several languages, but he knew it was better to speak only a few words others could understand than thousands they didn't understand (vv. 18, 19).

Paul's approach to speaking ought to be followed by all Christian workers who speak in public, whether pastors, Sunday Bible School teachers, youth leaders, children's church workers, club leaders or any other leaders. There simply is no substitute for communicating in clear, understandable language. A Christian speaker who drives his audience to their dictionaries more often than to their Bibles needs to learn from Paul—and from the Lord—who spoke profound truths in simple terms.

Tongues in Check

The Corinthian church's services must have resembled a three-ring circus at times, as various members felt led to sing, teach, prophesy, speak in unfamiliar languages and ask questions without any regard for order. Since God is orderly, His assembled people ought to worship in an orderly fashion. Paul limited the use of tongues in the Corinthian church to no more than three speakers in one service—and always in turn with the assistance of an interpreter. He prescribed the same order for speakers who prophesied (vv. 29–31).

Q4. Do you feel it helps or hinders a church's worship service to follow a prescribed order of worship? Explain.

_____

_____

_____

Verses 32 and 33 continue Paul's emphasis on order in church worship. Speakers were supposed to control themselves at all times, restraining any impulse to speak if someone else had the floor. In other words, a church service was not to become an emotionally charged meeting in which frenzy displaced the faith—objective truth.

What Tongues Told

What was the purpose of tongues (the supernatural ability to speak in unlearned foreign languages) in the first century? Tongues served to authenticate the gospel to unbelieving Jews. Verse 22a states: "Wherefore tongues are for a sign, not to them that believe, but to them that believe not."

The first occurrence of tongues in the New Testament was at Pentecost (Acts 2:1–11). Jews from around the world had come to Jerusalem to celebrate the Jewish festivals, including Pentecost. At Pentecost the apostles spoke in languages native to the international audience, and many Jews, upon hearing the gospel in their own language, trusted in their Messiah. This and other occurrences of speaking in tongues fulfilled God's promise to the Jews that He would speak to them with other tongues (Isa. 28:11; 1 Cor. 14:21).

Hold Your Questions 'Til Dinner

Paul's final words to the Corinthians about an orderly worship service included instructions to the women of the church. They were to refrain from speaking in a service (1 Cor. 14:34). Their compliance with this command would show their compliance with God's will (v. 34b). If a woman had questions about a doctrinal truth, she was obliged to wait until she could ask her husband at home (v. 35). Obviously, this instruction obligated the Corinthian husbands to know God's truth and help their wives grow in grace and knowledge. Although most Christian women today are well-educated and many are well-versed in the Word of God, husbands still have a responsibility to contribute to their wives' spiritual well-being.

Q5. Was the teaching that women should be silent in church strictly a cultural consideration? Why or why not?

_____

_____

_____

_____

The Corinthian church had no right to act in a disruptive, do-your-own-thing kind of way. It wasn't a law unto itself. It had neither originated the Scriptures nor been the only church to receive the Scriptures (v. 36). Like all the other churches, it was obligated to obey God's Word and not rewrite it. Paul's instructions and commands—his very words—to the Corinthians were from the Lord (v. 37). Whoever rejected those words would remain ignorant (v. 38). However, Paul wanted the Corinthians to grow strong spiritually, desire to proclaim the truth, allow the gift of tongues (properly exercised for God's intended purpose at the time) and do all things "decently and in order" (vv. 39, 40).

Time for Action

• Since God desires orderly worship, organize your thoughts for Sunday worship. Take a few notes during each church service to express your love for God, your gratitude for His character and works, the help received from the message and the ways you intend to serve Him in the coming week.

• Worship God privately every day by focusing your mind and your heart upon God, as the Bible portrays Him.

• Set a good example of reverential worship by participating wholeheartedly in the worship service of your church and by refraining from unnecessary conversation.

• The gift of tongues vanished when the New Testament was completed. What importance do you attach to declaring New Testament truth to the unsaved? Share the plan of salvation with at least one person this week.

• If you are a husband or a wife, help your spouse to grow spiritually this week.

12 Up from the Grave!

† 1 Corinthians 15

Because Christ lives, we, too, shall live.

Centuries before Jesus Christ walked in Galilee, Job posed life's most penetrating question: "If a man die, shall he live again?" (Job 14:14). First Corinthians 15 answers Job's question decisively and dramatically. "But now is Christ risen from the dead, and become the firstfruits of them that slept" (1 Cor. 15:20).

Good News to Proclaim

In their frenzied desire for spectacular gifts, some of the Corinthians had lost sight of basic doctrine. A love for sensationalism had displaced a love for Scripture. Today, too, some churches seem to care more about excitement than edification. "Come to a show," seems to be the subtle invitation of some churches, when people ought to be invited to come and grow. The Bible is replaced by everything from ballet to ballyhoo.

Some Corinthians had denied the doctrine of the resurrection of the dead, although they professed to believe in Christ's resurrection (v. 12). In order to correct their erroneous view, Paul took them back to basics, beginning with the doctrinal components of the gospel.

The gospel Paul had declared in Corinth about five years before he wrote 1 Corinthians contained the following truths: 1) "Christ died for our sins according to the scriptures" (v. 3). God's Son paid the penalty of our sins at Calvary, and He did so in fulfillment of the Old Testament prophecies about His suffering for sin. 2) "He was buried" (v. 4). Jesus' dead body was laid to rest in a tomb belonging to Joseph of Arimathea. 3) "He rose again the third day according to the scriptures" (v. 4). 4) "He was seen" (v. 5). The gospel, then, presents a crucified, buried and risen Savior, Who fulfilled Scripture and appeared in risen form to eyewitnesses.

> *Q1. What doctrine did Paul link to the resurrection of Christ in Romans 4:25? How does this doctrine affect our relationship with God?*

_____

_____

_____

First, Paul named Peter ("Cephas") as an eyewitness (1 Cor. 15:5). Next, he named the Twelve (v. 5),

---

Grow in Grace . . .

"But now is Christ risen from the dead, and become the firstfruits of them that slept" (1 Cor. 15:20).

Christ's resurrection guarantees a harvest of resurrected believers unto life and of unbelievers unto condemnation (John 5:28, 29). As you memorize and meditate on 1 Corinthians 15:20, thank God for your salvation, and reach out to others with His love.

112

. . . and Knowledge

*Read these related
Scriptures as you study
1 Corinthians 15 this week.*

Job 19:23–27
Psalm 16
Romans 8:18–25
1 Thessalonians 4:13–18
1 Peter 1:3–9

meaning the disciples collectively (Mark 16:14). After this, he wrote that a gathering of more than 500 believers saw the risen Christ. Some of them were still alive when Paul wrote 1 Corinthians (1 Cor. 15:6). Then he referred to two more eyewitness experiences. He wrote that James (possibly the Lord's half brother) saw the risen Lord, and the Twelve saw Him again (v. 7). Finally, Paul named himself as an eyewitness (v. 8), and he reminded his readers that he had persecuted the church before he met the risen Lord. But after meeting Him, by the grace of God he became the Lord's most zealous apostle (vv. 9, 10).

Q2. Why are eyewitnesses crucial in deciding a court case?

_____

_____

_____

The Corinthians, too, had felt the impact of Christ's resurrection. Upon hearing the gospel, they had believed on Christ (v. 11).

An Empty Tomb or an Empty Life

Christ's resurrection guarantees ours. Those who deny the possibility of a bodily resurrection must also deny that Christ arose from the grave (vv. 12, 13).

If Christ did not rise from the grave, all preaching is

113

futile, simply empty words offering empty hope based on empty promises and empty claims. If there was no resurrection, Christ wasn't Deity and the Bible isn't God's reliable Word. Furthermore, if there wasn't a resurrection, faith in Christ is ill-founded and believers are still lost in sin (vv. 14–17).

The scenario continues. If Christ did not arise from the dead, departed believers have entered an eternal Hell (v. 18), and living believers ought to be most pitied (v. 19). After all, it is one thing to endure persecutions and deprivation for the sake of a risen Christ, but it is quite another to endure such trials for the sake of a lie.

That Big Little Word "but"

"But now is Christ risen from the dead . . . ," Paul assured the Corinthians (v. 20a). There is a valid gospel to proclaim. There is hope, life beyond the grave, the prospect of reunion with departed Christian loved ones and a reason to endure persecution. Drawing from Leviticus 23:10, Paul exclaimed that Christ has "become the firstfruits of them that slept" (1 Cor. 15:20b). As death came to all by Adam, so life came to all who are in Christ (v. 21).

> Q3. Read 1 Peter 1:3. *What has the resurrection of Christ produced in Christians? How is this demonstrated in daily living?*
>
> _____
>
> _____
>
> _____

The order of the resurrection and other future events appears in verses 23–28:
1. Christ's resurrection.
2. Believers' resurrection at His coming (Church Age

believers at the Rapture, all other believers at the Second Coming).

3. Christ's reign, which includes the subjection of all authorities to Himself and the final destruction of death.

4. Deliverance of a completely redeemed creation to God.

5. The supremacy of God over all.

The resurrection of Christ made baptism meaningful. Paul viewed the ranks of Christians as soldiers engaged in spiritual warfare. As some Christian soldiers died, others stepped in to take their place. In baptism, these new believers confessed their faith in Christ and allegiance to Him (v. 29).

The resurrection made Paul's perilous life worthwhile. He faced death daily for the sake of the gospel, having turned his back on the allurements of a soft and carefree life (vv. 30–32). His reference to fighting wild beasts at Ephesus may be to the wild public demonstration against him when he preached there (Acts 19:23–34). Sometimes, human foes of the gospel can act like vicious animals, as church history shows.

In 1 Corinthians 15:33 and 34, Paul called upon the Corinthian Christians to turn away from false teachers who denied the resurrection.

Q4. Why is it important to separate ourselves from all forms of apostasy?

_____

_____

_____

Questions about the Resurrection

Do you wonder how the resurrection will take place and what the resurrection body will look like? Some of the Corinthians entertained similar questions. "How are the dead raised up? and with what body do they come?" (v. 35). Here's what Paul told them.

He compared death and resurrection to the planting of seeds. When a seed is buried in the ground, it dies; but ultimately it produces new life in the form of a plant (vv. 36–38). Likewise, in the resurrection God will produce a brand-new body from the old one, even though the old one may have decomposed.

Furthermore, Paul explained, all plants are not alike. God has designed each plant with distinct characteristics. According to 1 Corinthians 15:39–41, there are different kinds of bodies. There are human bodies and bodies of animals. Fish have their distinct bodies, and birds have theirs. Paul pointed to the difference between heavenly bodies (sun, moon, stars) and earthly bodies (men, animals, fish, birds). Since God gave a distinct glory to each heavenly body, He can be trusted to give the resurrection body distinct features (vv. 41, 42a).

The believer's resurrection body will be a glorified version of his earthly body. It will be a real body—incorruptible, spiritual, eternal and fashioned after Jesus' resurrection body (vv. 42b–44; Rom. 8:11, 23, 30; 2 Cor. 5:1; Phil. 3:21). It will be impervious to sickness, disease and dying (Rev. 21:4). There will be no more arthritic pain, migraine headaches, heart problems, diabetes, kidney disease, ulcers, bad lower backs or hardening of the arteries. Our feet won't hurt; our nerves won't pinch; and our joints won't ache. We will never grow tired, irritable or old. Doctor bills and four-a-day pills will be things of the past. We won't need cosmetic surgery, cosmetic dentistry or cosmetic products; yet we'll look better in Heaven than we ever did on earth.

We owe this bright outlook to Jesus Christ. God formed the first Adam from the earth and made him a living soul. The Lord came from Heaven to give life to

Adam's fallen race. Those who trust in Christ are made alive in Christ, and each of them will possess a glorified body someday (1 Cor. 15:45–49). In Romans 8:29 Paul anticipated this culmination of our redemption. He announced: "For whom he did foreknow, he also did predestinate to be conformed to the image of his Son, that he might be the firstborn among many brethren."

Unless a person has a spiritual dimension to his life by being born again, he cannot inherit the kingdom of God (1 Cor. 15:50). Flesh and blood are unsuitable for a heavenly, eternal life. As Jesus told Nicodemus, a Pharisee and a ruler of the Jews, "Except a man be born again, he cannot see the kingdom of God" (John 3:3).

Many in our time need to learn the importance and necessity of being born again. Modern man puts a high value on physical health and fitness but little or no value on spiritual health and fitness. He spends money, time and energy in the pursuit of body care but neglects the care of his soul. Yet the soul is eternal, whereas even the best conditioned body wears out and dies. Is it any wonder Jesus warned, "For what is a man profited, if he shall gain the whole world, and lose his own soul? or what shall a man give in exchange for his soul?" (Matt. 16:26).

Mystery Writer

"Behold, I shew you a mystery," Paul wrote (1 Cor. 15:51a). The Biblical meaning of the word "mystery" is a divine disclosure of previously unknown truth. In this case, the truth focused on what happens to Christians at the Rapture, the return of Christ in the air to remove His church from earth to Heaven. At that time, the bodies of living Christians will be transformed into the likeness of Christ's body. These Christians will not experience death. "We shall not all sleep, but we shall all be changed," Paul explained (v. 51b).

The bodies of dead Christians will be changed at the Rapture too. It will happen quicker than the shortest measure of time ("a moment") and the flutter of an eyelash (v. 52a). The last trumpet will sound, and the graves of dead Christians will burst open. The bodies in the graves will experience resurrection. They will rocket to the skies, undergoing a dramatic and dynamic change on the way up. Those decomposing and decomposed bodies will become incorruptible (v. 52).

Just what is the last trumpet? Some Bible teachers relate it to a use of the trumpet in Old Testament times to convene celebrations such as the year of Jubilee (Lev. 25:9). The year of Jubilee brought freedom to those who were in bondage. Families were reunited, and debts were canceled. Certainly, when the trumpet sounds at the Rapture (1 Thess. 4:16), we will enter into the greatest freedom we human beings can know. We will be free forever from the allurements of the world, the flesh and the Devil.

Perhaps Paul's reference to "the last trump" in 1 Corinthians 15:52 sprang from the use of the trumpet in first-century Roman military procedure. The first trumpet signal notified the Roman soldiers it was time to break camp. The second trumpet call announced it was time to fall into line for the march. The last trumpet signaled the beginning of the march. At the Rapture, we Christians will depart from earth where we have pitched our tents. We will follow our Commander in Chief, the Lord Jesus, to our heavenly destination.

At the Rapture, Christ, Who destroyed death and defeated the grave, will give dead Christians incorruptible bodies and living Christians immortal bodies (v. 53). Death will be swallowed up in victory (v. 54; Isa. 25:8).

It Won't Even Sting!

By grace, Christians share Christ's victory over death.

We have no more to fear from this defeated foe than from a bee whose stinger has been removed. Christ took the sting out of death! Paul asks triumphantly, "O death, where is thy sting? O grave, where is thy victory?" (v. 55).

Adam's sin resulted in death for the human race, and the law always revealed sin (v. 56), but Christ has set believers free from sin's penalty and power. At the Rapture, Christians will be free from sin's presence as well. Just the thought of this deliverance caused Paul to offer jubilant thanks to "God, which giveth us the victory through our Lord Jesus Christ" (v. 57).

Let's Work while We Wait

We do not know when the Rapture will occur, but it could occur in our lifetime. Since this possibility is real, we may not have much longer to wait for Christ or to work for Him on this earth. Paul's challenge to the Corinthians extends to us too. Let us be "stedfast," never swerving from the goal of doing God's will; "unmoveable," never swerving from the faith; and "always abounding in the work of the Lord," never lagging in our commitment to Christ but always energetically serving Him (v. 58a).

While driving in the hills of Pennsylvania a number of years ago, I got behind a truck with an interesting slogan placarded across its back doors. It announced: "Any load. Any time. Anywhere." I asked myself if I was willing at any time to carry any load the Lord placed on me to any destination He chose. What good things would result if everyone in your local church adopted that slogan? Our labor is not in vain in the Lord (v. 58b)! Christ's resurrection proves it.

Time for Action

• The gospel is good news to be shared. Share it with

others this week. If you don't normally have contact with unsaved people, pray that God will bring those prepared by Him into your life this week.

• Paul's life demonstrated the power of Christ's resurrection. What aspects of your daily living reflect your union with the risen Christ? Are there areas of your life that need attention?

• Consider the possibility that the Rapture might take place in your lifetime. What positive action will you take in view of this possibility?

• Are you about ready to throw in the towel as far as Christian service is concerned? If you are, let the fact that Christ is alive rekindle your zeal. Your labor is not in vain in the Lord.

13 A Heart for Giving

† 1 Corinthians 16

*Every Christian should give faithfully
to the Lord's work.*

The Sea of Galilee receives water at the north from the Jordan and dispenses it at the south, as the Jordan flows on. Fish are plentiful in this sea. The Dead Sea, too, receives water from the Jordan, but the sea retains it. As a result, this sea's water is stagnant and unproductive. It is well named the Dead Sea. Like the Sea of Galilee, believers who give generously in proportion to what they receive from the Lord lead productive lives. Like the Dead Sea, some believers selfishly keep what they receive, and their lives become stagnant and unproductive.

In his closing remarks to the Corinthians, Paul challenged them to honor God by practicing faithful stewardship.

A Relief Project

Christians in Jerusalem were poor, perhaps because of the intense persecution there. Yet they were not forgotten. Paul established a relief fund for them among the churches of Galatia and Macedonia. In 1 Corinthians 16:1, he appealed to the Corinthian church to participate in the cause. He wrote: "Now concerning

121

the collection for the saints, as I have given order to the churches of Galatia, even so do ye."

> Q1. Read 1 John 3:16–18. *How does this passage relate to 1 Corinthians 16:1?*

_____

_____

_____

A Plan for Giving

Paul led the Corinthians into a sensible and Scriptural plan for giving. Upon the first day of the week, the Lord's Day, everyone in the church was to give as God had prospered him. This would eliminate the need of a special offering when Paul visited Corinth (v. 2).

This simple but effective plan is on target for Christians of every generation. It should be adopted individually and followed diligently for the sake of the Lord's work and personal spiritual development. By giving on the Lord's Day, we associate the act of giving with worship. Our offering becomes a way of ackowledging that God is great and good. We show that we love Him and seek to honor Him. Also, by

---

Grow in Grace . . .

"Upon the first day of the week let every one of you lay by him in store, as God hath prospered him, that there be no gatherings when I come" (1 Cor. 16:2).

As you memorize this verse, meditate on it. Examine your record of giving in the light of what God has given you.

. . . and Knowledge

*Read these related
Scriptures as you study
1 Corinthians 16 this week.*

Malachi 3:8–11
Matthew 6:19–34
Luke 19:12–27
2 Corinthians 8:1–15
2 Corinthians 9:6–15

giving on the first day of the week, we avoid the risk of giving haphazardly to the Lord's work. Our giving becomes systematic instead of spasmodic. Faithfulness rather than feelings governs our giving.

Every person in the Corinthian church received Paul's instruction to participate in the offering for the impoverished Jerusalem believers. "Let every one of you lay by him in store," Paul wrote (v. 2). A Christian may not be able to sing or preach or teach, but he can give—as a way of helping the ministry of the gospel at home and abroad. First, however, he should give himself to the Lord. The Macedonian believers did this. Paul told the Corinthians about this in 2 Corinthians 8:2–5: "How that in a great trial of affliction the abundance of their joy and their deep poverty abounded unto the riches of their liberality. For to their power, I bear record, yea, and beyond their power they were willing of themselves; praying us with much intreaty that we would receive the gift, and take upon us the fellowship of the ministering to the saints. And this they did, not as we hoped, but first gave their own selves to the Lord, and unto us by the will of God."

A church member refused to participate in an offering for missions. When an usher passed the offering plate to him, the miserly member muttered gruffly, "I'm not putting anything in; I don't believe in missions."

"Then take something out," the usher replied, "it's for the heathen."

Although every Christian ought to give to the Lord's work, some can give more than others. Paul wrote that every man should give "as God hath prospered him" (1 Cor. 16:2). Although he did not specify a percentage, surely ten percent—the tithe—is at least the acceptable starting point. Through His servant, Malachi, God indicted Israel with the crime of robbing Him by withholding tithes and offerings from Him. "Will a man rob God?" He asked the nation. "Yet ye have robbed me," He charged. Then, anticipating Israel's question, "Wherein have we robbed thee?" He explained, "In tithes and offerings" (Mal. 3:8). Christians who give as God has prospered them will not be indicted with the crime of robbery! On the positive side, they will experience the joy that obedience kindles, and they will enjoy God's approval. Luke 6:38 promises, "Give, and it shall be given unto you; good measure, pressed down, and shaken together, and running over, shall men give into your bosom. For with the same measure that ye mete withal it shall be measured to you again."

Q2. Since God doesn't need anything, why does He ask His people to give?

_____

_____

_____

A Plan for Handling the Offering

The Corinthians' offering for the poor Christians in Jerusalem deserved careful and respectful handling. Paul avoided any possibility of criticism by asking the Corinthian church to select the men who would carry the offering to Jerusalem (1 Cor. 16:3). If it was necessary for Paul to accompany them, he would do so (v. 4).

Many churches believe it is wise to appoint more

than one trusted individual to count the offerings. Also, they follow an accounting system that includes periodic audits and prevents indiscriminate writing of checks. Fortunately, their treasurers appreciate such careful procedures, knowing it safeguards their reputations and honors the stewardship of God's people.

Q3. What characteristics are essential in those who handle church funds?

_____

_____

_____

When Opportunity Knocks

Some years before writing to the Corinthians, Paul had learned to be sensitive to the leading of the Holy Spirit. Paul's plan called for an evangelistic trip into Asia, but God's plan at the time called for the evangelization of Europe (Acts 16:6–12). When he realized the direction God wanted him to take, he wasted no time in going that way.

First Corinthians 16:5–9 reveals Paul's willingness to subject his will to the Lord's. He intended to seize the opportunities the Lord placed before him. He planned to visit Corinth and possibly spend the winter there, but this was subject to the Lord's will (v. 7b). In the meantime he would stay at Ephesus until Pentecost because the Lord had given him a wide door of opportunity for ministry there (v. 9a). Many adversaries opposed Paul's ministry, but they could not uproot him from the place of God's appointment (v. 9b).

Q4. What opportunities has the Lord given our church?

_____

_____

Commendations and Exhortations

Paul commended Timothy to the Corinthians. He had sent Timothy to Corinth (1 Cor. 4:17) and expected him to arrive there soon. Paul urged the Corinthians to treat Timothy kindly and respectfully, because Timothy "worketh the work of the Lord, as I also do," Paul assured the Corinthians (1 Cor. 16:10).

Apparently, some people took advantage of Timothy's youthfulness and timid personality. Paul didn't want that to happen in Corinth. He commanded the Corinthians: "Let no man . . . despise him" (v. 11a). Instead of despising Timothy, the Corinthians were urged to help him get back to Paul, who was looking forward to Timothy's return (v. 11b). Like Timothy, many young adults today are performing the work of the Lord and deserve the respect and cooperation of the Lord's people.

Although a faction in the church at Corinth preferred Apollos over Paul and another preferred Paul over Apollos, these two servants esteemed each other highly. Paul wasn't jealous of Apollos. He wanted Apollos to visit the Corinthian church. It appears Apollos didn't want his presence in Corinth to fuel the cause of the Apollos clique, so he chose to stay away for the time being (v. 12).

Paul exhorted the Corinthians to be alert, maintain the faith and be courageous and strong (v. 13). They were to let love govern all their actions (v. 14). The Stephanas family, the first converts in Achaia, where Corinth was located, had given themselves completely to the task of serving God's people (v. 15). Paul urged the Corinthians to submit to such outstanding Christian workers (v. 16).

As a matter of fact, Stephanas, along with Fortunatus and Achaicus, had gone from Corinth to Ephesus to visit Paul. The purpose of the journey was to supply

Paul with something the Corinthian church had failed to give him (v. 17). These brothers in Christ knew how to minister to others. They lifted Paul's spirit, just as they had lifted the spirits of the Corinthians (v. 18a). Paul urged the Corinthians to give these men the recognition they deserved (v. 18b).

In sending greetings from the churches in Asia to the church at Corinth, Paul identified two of the greeters: Aquila and Priscilla. They sent especially warm regards, and the church in their house joined them in doing so (v. 19). Since Aquila and Priscilla had lived in Corinth (Acts 18:1–3), they must have known many of the Corinthian Christians well.

Aquila and Priscilla were a hospitable couple. The New Testament traces their travels from Rome to Corinth to Ephesus and finally back to Rome. Wherever they settled, they served the Lord diligently and opened their home for discipleship and worship. Churches today are fortunate if they have couples like Aquila and Priscilla in their membership. A home open for hospitable fellowship and service provides a haven and a little bit of Heaven for all who enter its doors.

Q5. How have you been blessed by the hospitality of a dedicated Christian couple?

_____

_____

_____

A Warm Farewell

Some members of the Corinthian church may not have appreciated Paul or been willing to submit to his apostolic authority, but the Christians at Ephesus stood with Paul, and Paul loved the Corinthians in spite of their unruliness. He passed along greetings from the Ephesian Christians and told the Corinthians to greet one another with a holy kiss (v. 20). It would require a mini-revival to get some Corinthians to kiss their fellow church members, but Paul was confident this could happen—and would happen. If the Corinthians exchanged kisses with one another, they would be far less likely to exchange mean words.

Paul closed 1 Corinthians with a signature, a warning and a benediction. The letter was so important Paul signed his name to it (v. 21). Apparently he didn't want anyone to suggest it hadn't come from him. He warned that, if anyone did not love Christ, he should be accursed. Indeed, at the Lord's coming, He will reject all who rejected Him (v. 22). For all the Corinthian Christians, however, Paul offered a benediction of grace and love (vv. 23, 24). Divine grace would help the Corinthians solve their problems and practice right worship, and Paul's love would make it easier for them to heed his words.

Time for Action

• How can you improve your giving to the Lord's work? Do you give with a pure motive?

• What opportunities has the Lord given you for Christian witness and service? How will you respond to these opportunities this week?

• If you feel timid about doing the Lord's work, how can you be encouraged by Timothy's example?

• How will you use your home for Christian witness and fellowship?

• How can you encourage a Christian worker this week?